HUMPHRY DAVY

and Chemical Discovery

Sir Humphry Davy

IMMORTALS OF SCIENCE

HUMPHRY DAVY

and Chemical Discovery

Elba O. Carrier

Franklin Watts, Inc.
575 Lexington Avenue
New York, N.Y. 10022

FIRST PRINTING
Copyright © 1965 by Franklin Watts, Inc.
Library of Congress Catalog Card Number 65-11751
Printed in the United States of America

U. S.   1466514

Contents

CHAPTER ONE

An Appeal to Science for Help

Just before noon on May 25, 1812, the whole earth seemed to quiver and shake near Sunderland, England. A huge black cloud appeared with the suddenness of night and a mysterious twilight covered the countryside.

Some of the superstitious countryfolk were awestruck. "Is it the end of the world?" they asked each other. Many fell in fear and prayer or simply stood bewildered, awaiting the end.

Not so the wives and children of the miners' families. They set off frantically toward the mouths of the pits at Felling Colliery. The great cloud of black was frightening to them also, but in quite another way. For the rumble of the earth could only mean that there had been an explosion in the coal mines.

Near the mouth of the pit, the coal dust in the air was a choking barrier, but the desperate relatives of the men trapped below forced their way forward. A ring

I

was formed to prevent them getting so near that they would be in the way of rescue attempts. The explosion had shattered all the mechanical equipment, but men in desperate haste were lowering ropes into the open maw.

Someone screamed, "They're all dead!"

By now the crowd was nearly panicked. In this English coal country, people lived under the shadow of the disaster that could overcome their menfolk—a daily dread that their men would not return from the bowels of the earth. In 1812 the growing demands of the industrial revolution for more and more power had brought about efforts to increase the supply of coal, and many new mines had been opened. Old mines were pushed deeper into the earth. The stories of mine explosions were becoming frequent.

The rescuers worked their first rope to the surface and a grinning black figure scrambled to his feet. Word went back through the crowd, spreading hope. "They're bringing them up. They're coming!"

Thirty-two survivors out of the one hundred and twenty-four trapped miners were brought up by one o'clock. Then no more appeared. Volunteers went down to check passages in the other chambers for the remaining ninety-two men. People whose relatives had not yet been found began to feel their hopes fade. A new and dismal note was added when three of the rescued men died very soon after being saved.

At two o'clock another blast shattered the prayerful quiet of the waiting multitude, and the smoke which emptied from the mine pit indicated that the mine was now burning and would soon endanger the whole countryside. Despite the cries of "Murder!" from the anguished relatives, the mine was sealed. Six weeks later a crew reopened the mine, and the bodies of the ninety-two victims were found, scorched and seared. It was plain that they had been killed at the first moment of the original blast.

The growing public distress over this catastrophe, and others like it, began to sweep over the land. Naturally, the appalling loss of lives disturbed people in coal mining communities, but now individuals in virtually all parts of England and Wales were also gravely troubled. The owners of the mines themselves were greatly disturbed, not only because of the danger to the workers but also because idle mines could not produce, and increased dangers meant increased expenditures.

Ministers talked of the tragedies from their pulpits, and groups of people began to form to consider what might be done. One such group was called "The Society for Preventing Accidents in Coal Mines." This group had written to various experts to request advice on the measures their society should consider. John Buddle, who was an authority on coal mine ventilation, had written to point out that they must turn to scientific men to find a remedy.

The president of the group, Mr. Wilkinson, a lawyer, addressed the gathering. "Mr. Buddle is right. We must look to science to help us to eliminate these disasters. Where else then but to the foremost scientist in England? I propose to go to Sir Humphry Davy himself and request his assistance." The approval of the society was given by acclamation.

Today it is difficult for us to imagine how remarkable this appeal was. Science is now a part of everyone's life and fills our daily newspapers and magazines. Writers speak of science and what it can do, and scientists themselves appear on television, radio, and in our schools to tell us of their work. We have science classes in high school and in junior high, and many of us learn about science in the elementary grades.

In 1812, however, scientists and science were far from being well known or appreciated. Part of our story here is to point out the contribution to our knowledge by one man—a scientist in an age where science was in its infancy.

As it happened, Mr. Wilkinson was not able to see Humphry Davy until some time after the surprising interest was shown by "The Society for Preventing Accidents in Coal Mines." Sir Humphry had just left for a trip on the Continent, and it was not until he returned from France and Italy in 1815 that Mr. Wilkinson was able to reach him.

The story of how Humphry Davy did indeed attack

the problem of mine explosions will be told later. But it is significant to note that this one group at least turned to men of science for help at that time, hoping that the application of science to their problem would help mankind.

Moreover, it is a remarkable fact that Humphry Davy himself was only thirty-three years old when he was appealed to as the foremost chemist of his age. It is even more striking that only fifteen years before, in the year 1797, Humphry Davy, eighteen years of age and an orphan, had begun studying chemistry by himself, while apprenticed to a village doctor in the west of England.

This is the story of that boy and that man.

CHAPTER TWO

The Boyhood of Humphry Davy

Humphry Davy was born in Penzance, a town in Cornwall on the very westernmost tip of England, on December 17, 1778. He was the firstborn child of Robert and Grace Davy.

John Davy, Humphry's youngest brother and a well-known scientist himself, has written much about his brilliant older brother. He tells how their father recorded Humphry's birth in a large family Bible. We may wonder what dreams this proud father may have had for his son, but what actually transpired in Humphry's life was surely quite beyond his imagining at the time.

The Davy family had been established in Cornwall for over two hundred and fifty years and, although not a wealthy family, they were not poor. Humphry's father was a wood-carver and some of his work—such as the superb mantelpiece in the Ludgvan Rectory—still

6

stands today. Ludgvan was a farming community three miles from Penzance where the Davy family farm called Varfell was located.

Humphry Davy's grandfather had been a successful builder and had apprenticed his youngest son Robert to a London wood-carver. After the death of his father, Robert inherited the farm and practiced his wood carving only as a hobby. The family moved from Penzance to Ludgvan and Humphry spent his boyhood partly at his father's farm but mostly in Penzance where he attended school and boarded with a surgeon, Dr. John Tonkin. Dr. Tonkin was a family friend of long standing. As a physician he had attended the Milletts, the parents of Humphry Davy's mother, during their fatal illnesses. Upon their deaths he had brought up Grace Millett as his only daughter.

Dr. Tonkin played a large part in Humphry's upbringing and was, moreover, somewhat of an eccentric. Although he required no repayment from the Davys, he kept an account book of his expenses for Humphry from 1784 until 1795. A strange old man, he loved children and was very kind and friendly. He was also quick-tempered. Later, Humphry's decision against becoming a doctor caused Dr. Tonkin great distress.

It was said that Dr. Tonkin went around the countryside taking care of his patients, helping the ill, the maimed, and the crippled, dressed in clothing that would have been in fashion in the previous century. He still wore a cocked hat, a large powdered wig, an upright collar, ruffles, and drove his carriage with the pride and conviction of a man sure of himself. He was eighty-two when he died.

Penzance was a beautiful and exciting place for Humphry Davy. It was a town of about three thousand people who were either farmers in the very lush countryside, fishermen on the coast, traders from community to community, or workers in the tin mines that abounded in the area. Humphry was a bright child and developed a reputation as a storyteller at an early age. His classmates would listen to him for hours. The material for his stories came from the many people with whom he spoke, and even more from the many places where he would walk, climb, and fish. For the boy knew well the whole of that beautiful country from Lands End (which was only ten miles from Penzance) all the way to the Lizard, with its stretching expanse of sea toward the south called Mounts Bay.

In telling his stories, Humphry drew on much of the lore of Cornish history, which he learned from the people he met. Even before the Romans marched across Cornwall, the ancient Phoenicians, those superb navigators of thousands of years ago, had pushed their ships through the Mediterranean and past Gibraltar into the wilder waters of the Atlantic. They had sailed up the coast of Portugal, Spain, and France to the shores of Britain. Here they found the bays and coves of Cornwall safe havens from the frequent gales, while they opened up trade lanes to the east for the rich tin and copper of the Cornwall Peninsula. This part of Cornwall, together with the Scilly Islands which are some thirty miles west of the Cornish coast, was known as the Cassiterides, or Tin Isles, by the Phoenicians and Greeks.

In his walks about the countryside, Humphry Davy would come upon spots which had been old Saxon camps. He would also pass remnants of the earthworks of the Danes and Saxons and explore the remains of ancient castles and monasteries. Marauding Spaniards burned Penzance to ashes and pillaged Mousehole and Paul in 1595. Later, in 1646, Penzance was sacked by Fairfax and then was sacked periodically until 1750 when Algerian pirates raided the coast of Cornwall. The marks left by these historical happenings were everywhere and few details escaped Humphry's eye. His Grandmother Davy told him stories that made him think of the land as alive with spirits. He would spend hours listening to these tales. She could talk of the elves in the woods, the pirates that scoured the seas, and the secret places in the forest where the trees whispered to each other.

She also told him much about his family. The reason Humphry had been left in Penzance with Dr. Tonkin was that he could attend a local preparatory school kept by a Mr. Bushell. Mr. Bushell was quite impressed with

Humphry Davy's talents and urged his father to send him to a more advanced school. Humphry then went to the Penzance Grammar School where the Reverend Mr. Coryton was the headmaster and teacher.

Humphry Davy's brother John has described Mr. Coryton as a man of irregular habits and ill fitted for the office of teaching youth. He pointed out the man's deficiency in good teaching methods and in instilling sound scholarship. He felt that he was, by turns, careless, indiscriminate, overcritical, harsh, and intolerant in trivial matters. On more than one occasion Humphry Davy got his ears pulled.

One day Humphry came to school with a large plaster on each ear and when Mr. Coryton asked what was wrong with his ears, he replied, "I put the plasters on to prevent a mortification." Mr. Coryton was not amused by this type of humor and consequently Humphry suffered a walloping with Mr. Coryton's flat ruler.

At this time Humphry Davy made little effort in school. Why should he have? With his excellent memory he could lead the class without studying, and even admitted later that he enjoyed idleness during this period. He was popular with his schoolmates, and one of his diversions was to excite his friends with stories adapted from his grandmother's about the miners and fishermen; or stories which he invented himself.

Humphry was also acknowledged to be the best youthful fisherman in the region. At Penzance pier he had devised a way to catch gray mullet, which none of the other boys could imitate. Because of the mullet's small mouth it is a difficult fish to catch, but Davy invented a technique by which he would snare several of them on a group of distributed hooks with a quick movement of his line. He also had a great admiration for people who were fishermen. In fact, his admiration of the great naval hero Horatio Nelson was partly due to the fact that the famous admiral had learned to cast a fly left-handed, after losing his right arm.

The background of Cornish superstition, and all of the fishing and roaming through the countryside, inspired Humphry to write poetry. Later, when he was eighteen years old, Davy was to turn to science. While these two activities seem far apart, they were not so in Humphry's case. Indeed, one seemed to lead to the other. For, ever since he had been a little boy—observing, wondering, speculating, predicting—he had been on the road which leads to science.

Thus it is not surprising that Humphry wrote poetry, that he fished and hunted like his father, that he avidly told stories of sailors, farmers, and miners, for the poet and lover of nature and the listener and storyteller are a clear part of Humphry the boy. What is surprising is that he did these things, and others, so well.

Humphry Davy went to the Penzance Grammar School until he was fourteen years old. At that time Dr. Tonkin transferred him to a school at Truro, the Truro

Grammar School, which was under the direction of a Mr. Cardew. While the school at Truro excited him when he first went there, it soon left him disappointed. Humphry wrote to his mother later regarding the education of his brother John. "I recollect I was rejoiced when I first went to Truro School, but I was much more rejoiced when I left it forever. Learning naturally is a true pleasure; how unfortunate then it is that in most schools it is made a pain. Yet Mr. Cardew comparatively was a most excellent master. I wish John may have as good a one."

Actually, Mr. Cardew favorably influenced the man who later became Sir Humphry Davy. However, he felt inclined to take little credit for this, although he was very pleased that he had encouraged Humphry Davy's interest in poetry.

Davy spent about a year at Truro and at the end of that time it was considered that his education was finished. Dr. Tonkin was still extremely interested in the boy and, as an indulgent foster father, encouraged him simply to enjoy himself. Thus a year passed which Humphry was later to look back on as virtually wasted time.

Nevertheless, Humphry Davy showed much interest in a variety of things. He took lessons in French from a refugee who had come to Penzance from France. At this time he also took up drawing and, although there is no evidence that he became very able, it probably helped him in sketching the experiments that he was later to describe.

The great jolt to young Humphry came when he was sixteen years old. On a mild winter's day in December of 1794, the kindly Dr. Tonkin returned from a call, wearing a grave face. Humphry was about to start off for the hills, and they ran into each other just outside the door.

It was still early. Humphry was so bright-eyed with anticipation that he did not notice Dr. Tonkin's worried expression. He said a cheery good morning, waved good-naturedly, and started down the street.

"Humphry!" Dr. Tonkin's voice was hoarse and uncertain.

Humphry turned slowly and stared at his guardian. "Are you ill?" He moved back toward him.

"No, no. I am fine, fine."

They stood there in the street. So natural did the country morning seem to Davy that he could not sense that this day was very different.

"Humphry," Dr. Tonkin began again, and hesitated.

"Yes?" Humphry was now quite perplexed.

Dr. Tonkin sighed. For so many years he had seen life come and go. It was never easy to tell someone else about a tragedy. Now he faced a boy he loved, and the news he had was bad.

"It's your father, Humphry," he said finally. The older Davy had been ill for some time.

"He's worse?"

"He's gone."

Humphrey stared for a moment. Then, as the realization began to sink in, his eyes clouded quickly. "My poor mother," he cried, and turning, he started at a run toward Varfell, three miles away.

Dr. Tonkin watched sadly. He saw the boy still carrying his hunting musket, running hard toward the edge of the town, shoulders quaking as he ran.

CHAPTER THREE

Davy Begins to Study Science

The death of Humphry Davy's father in 1794 not only left the family without income but also left a large debt from Robert Davy's investment failures. For Humphry the death of his father was a crushing blow; he was the oldest son, and John was only four years old. Humphry asked himself what he could do to help. In fact, what was he doing with his own life? What was he accomplishing?

It was plain that the past year he had spent in indolence was beginning to prey on him. Of course he missed his father and their hunting and fishing expeditions together. Also, the debts came as a surprise! Altogether they amounted to thirteen hundred pounds—a considerable fortune in those days.

Determined now to settle down and make something of his life, Humphry Davy wrote out a plan of study for himself in a notebook. Few sixteen-year-olds have ever sketched out such an ambitious plan. It included seven languages, logic, geography, physics, mechanics, history, and mathematics. It also included a section called "My Profession," consisting of such subjects as pharmacy, anatomy, surgery, and chemistry listed under the title. The hopes that Dr. Tonkin had for Humphry to become a doctor were already showing their influence.

Humphry Davy's brother John, in his biography, has transcribed verbatim the plan of study which the young Humphry Davy outlined for himself in 1795.

It is as follows:

1. Theology, or Religion;   Taught by Nature
   Ethics, or Moral Virtues   by Revelation
2. Geography
3. My Profession
   (1) Botany   (2) Pharmacy
   (3) Nosology (classification   (4) Anatomy
       of diseases)
   (5) Surgery   (6) Chemistry
4. Logic
5. Language
   (1) English   (2) French   (3) Latin
   (4) Greek   (5) Italian   (6) Spanish
   (7) Hebrew
6. Physics
   (1) The doctrines and properties of natural bodies
   (2) Of the operations of nature

(3) Of the doctrines of fluids
(4) Of the properties of organized matter
(5) Of the organization of matter
(6) Simple Astronomy
7. Mechanics
8. Rhetoric
9. History and Chronology
10. Mathematics

In February of 1795 Dr. Tonkin paid to have the boy apprenticed to Dr. Bingham Borlase, who was a surgeon-apothecary in Penzance. Dr. Tonkin hoped that Humphry would become a general practitioner, but Humphry's own ambition was already stirring. He began to look forward to possible graduation from the famous medical school at Edinburgh University and later to a high rank in the medical profession.

Dr. Borlase was a man of ability and was later to become a very distinguished physician. It is certain that Humphry benefited greatly from his experiences and conversations with him. Sixteen years later Borlase was to become the mayor of Penzance.

During Davy's apprenticeship it became apparent that he enjoyed the apothecary side of the business far more than the surgery. He began gathering geological specimens and doing his experiments in physics. Surprisingly enough, he also continued writing poetry.

In the year 1795 Humphry wrote a poem which he

called "The Sons of Genius," and some of the lines in it are a clear indication of Humphry's own dreams at this time. One of these reads, "Theirs is the glory of a lasting name." The poets Coleridge and Wordsworth later included this poem in their anthology. Humphry Davy was to become a close friend of these famous literary men.

Humphry grew meditative during this year, reading philosophy as well as writing poems. St. Michael's Mount, towering over the bay, was a favorite topic in his verse. From a lonely pile of rocks—the Gulval Carne—he could muse over his churning ideas, let his fancy run in verse, or permit the pressures of his ambitions to drive his vision to the very pinnacle of St. Michael's Mount.

Some of the lines from Humphry's poem are also very suggestive of his interests. One stanza begins, "While superstition rules the vulgar soul, forbids the energies of man to rise . . ." Did the sixteen-year-old Humphry realize the dangerous influence which superstition can have on man's efforts to reach beyond himself? A later stanza begins, "To scan the laws of nature, to explore . . . on Newtonian wings." This suggests that Humphry may have already felt the power of the scientific approach—exploring the laws of nature as had the great Isaac Newton. What can these lines extracted from a boyhood poem tell us about Humphry Davy's inner thoughts? They may suggest that not only did he possess an inborn love of science, but that he also recognized that superstition was a kind of opposite of science.

Davy had always been interested in rocks. The granite of the hills is often worn by the weather into differently shaped blocks, piled in gigantic cairns. Humphry carried a rock hammer with him in his walks with Dr. Borlase, for he was always eager to add to his collection. He also explored many of the tin and copper mines. The tin and copper veins running through the granite and sandstone varied from a few inches to thirty feet thick. How deep they ran no one knew. Today these mines still produce a large part of England's mineral ore. Humphry had found that tin also occurs in the gravel, and he had seen lead, silver, cobalt, and antimony veins in the sandstone. Humphry had observed that Lizard Point had consisted of mica, slate, with soapstone veins and china stones, and he had collected specimens of serpentine and hornblende.

It is significant to note that one of Humphry's duties when he later became connected with the Royal Institution was to build up a large mineral collection. He then spent several months traveling about this same English countryside collecting and cataloging geological materials.

But it was in chemistry that Humphry Davy was later to distinguish himself. Although he did not begin to study chemistry until he was nineteen years old, there were signs of his interest earlier. There are some reports that he carried out spectacular experiments in the garret of Dr. Tonkin's house while he lived there. Humphry's sister often helped him during these weird experiments and she later complained of the "ravages committed on my dress by corrosive substance." The boys in Penzance often marveled at some of the explosive material which Humphry devised. Dr. Tonkin also marveled in a different way at the explosive sounds he heard in his own attic. "Good heavens," he would say, "that boy is impossible. He will blow us all into the air."

Nevertheless, Dr. Tonkin was proud of the boy. Years later, after Humphry Davy was knighted by the Prince Regent, he was to remember that Dr. Tonkin had often fondly addressed him as "Sir Humphry" while he lived there. "Sir Humphry, the explosive boy" did in reality become Sir Humphry as a grown man.

During 1796 there is evidence that Humphry Davy spent a great deal of time studying physics. One of his school friends, returning to Penzance from Cambridge for his vacation, during a discussion with Davy was startled at the extent to which Humphry had pushed his learning.

During the end of that year it appears that Davy concentrated even more heavily on geology. This fitted in well with his desire to roam the countryside, to collect rock specimens, to fish, to hunt. Later, when shown a drawing of the scenery around one of the mines not far from Penzance, Davy said, "How often as a boy have I wandered about those rocks in search of new minerals and when fatigued sat down upon the turf and exercised my fancy and anticipations of scientific renown."

It was not until the end of 1797, perhaps November or December, that Humphry Davy turned to the study of chemistry. He had only two books on the subject at this time. They were *Nicholson's Dictionary of Chemistry* and a translation of *Lavoisier's Elements of Chemistry* by Kerr. The first of these two books was only a collection of facts and opinion. In the second book, however, it was possible to watch the operation of one of the great scientific minds of the century. It was in this volume that the great Antoine Lavoisier reported the overthrowing of the phlogiston theory. Humphry Davy was thunderstruck when he read this material. The phlogiston theory had been twisted by new discoveries to mean that when substances burned they were supposed to have lost a material of negative weight. While this now seems rather ridiculous, at that time maintaining a hypothesis which had been previously quite successful was usually worth the effort. In this case, however, Lavoisier was able to develop his own brilliant theory of combustion, which suggests that when substances burn they combine with the oxygen in the air. This is why the discovery of oxygen, and the report of its discovery to Lavoisier by the English chemist Joseph Priestley, was so important.

The great Joseph Black of Edinburgh had been one of

Lavoisier's earliest advocates. However, he expressed some doubts about the complete refutation of the phlogiston theory since he felt that Lavoisier's explanation would fail in experiments with light. Humphry Davy was delighted to discover these two points of view and he set out with the greatest of enthusiasm to eliminate all problems. He began a series of experiments to test the ideas that he was beginning to develop in his studies concerning the nature of heat and light. His apparatus was limited, but he did have certain chemicals available in Dr. Borlase's apothecary.

Davy's progress was rapid. In a few months he found himself with new speculations, new ideas, and definite experiments already in his background. He was confident enough to devise an entirely new theory. It was his notion that his experiments had demonstrated how wrong the French school was.

At about this same time, near the end of the year 1797, Humphry Davy was to meet two friends who would have a profound influence on him the rest of his life. One of these friends was Gregory Watt, the son of James Watt, famous for his invention of the steam engine.

After her husband's death, Humphry Davy's mother had moved back to Penzance and opened a small millinery shop in the town and, in order to increase the family income, she also took in boarders. One of these was Gregory Watt, then a young man of twenty-one. Watt was attending the University of Glasgow and, due to poor health, had come to spend the winter in this warmer climate. Among the physicians who had recommended this move was Dr. Thomas Beddoes, a friend of his father.

Watt was a bright, earnest young man, two years older than Humphry Davy. He had been studying chemistry and geology at Glasgow University and at first, upon meeting Davy, was very scornful of the cocky younger man who could dare to "demolish the entire French theory of combustion in a half hour." Still, Watt listened to Davy and he soon recognized the brilliant and shrewd reasoning power that Davy could bring to bear on a problem. In time they became close friends and Gregory Watt remained in Penzance until the spring of 1798.

Davy and Watt soon found that they had many common interests. John Davy has reported that they met daily, exploring the country together, visiting the mines and returning from their treks through the countryside with pouches full of rock and mineral specimens. One of the mines, the famous Wherry Mine, had a shaft which was sunk in the sea and which had to be approached by a long wooden bridge. The workings of this mine were entirely underwater. It naturally excited Gregory Watt to see attached to the water pump a steam engine, so recently invented by his own father. Although Watt was never to recover from tuberculosis and was to die, still young, in 1804, he did have the satisfaction of seeing his friend Humphry Davy started well on his way to fame.

The second friend whom Davy made was Mr. Davies Gilbert, the man who was later to become Humphry's successor as President of the Royal Society. Davies Gilbert had been a student of Dr. Thomas Beddoes and was in frequent communication with him at Bristol.

Gilbert's first sight of Davy was an interesting one, as related by Davy's biographers. The story goes that Gilbert was walking with a friend when he passed Dr. Borlase's house and noticed a young man swinging on a gate, making the most humorous facial contortions. When he asked who that extraordinary fellow was, he was told it was young Davy, the carver's son, who was said to be fond of making chemical experiments. Now Davies Gilbert was a Cornish gentleman, a man of wealth and position, who had a very deep interest in science. "Chemical experiments!" he exclaimed in great surprise. "If that would be the case, I must have some conversation with him."

Gilbert went over and spoke to the young man and was impressed by what he saw and heard. In fact, he began to visit him frequently, inviting Davy to use his own library at his home at Tredrea, which was not far from Penzance. Gilbert also took him to see many of the people in the surrounding areas who were to encourage Davy in experimenting and exploring. One of these visits was to Dr. Edwards at the Hale copper works. It was here that Humphry Davy had his first look at a well-equipped laboratory. The young man was deeply impressed at the sight of certain chemical apparatus which he had heretofore known only through diagrams in books. Davy seemed particularly excited when he examined an air pump. As he handled the finely worked piece of equipment, he marveled that such a clever instrument could be constructed.

Early in 1798 Gregory Watt sent an account of Davy's researches on heat and light to Dr. Thomas Beddoes at Bristol. This was Dr. Beddoes' first knowledge of Humphry Davy. The following year he was to publish Davy's extraordinary theory of light, an act which Davy, though happy about it at the time, was to bitterly regret for the rest of his life. In this paper Davy challenged Lavoisier's supposition that light and heat were cause and effect and suggested experiments to show that there was no interdependence between them.

Early that same year Humphry Davy reported that his attention was directed to the "dephlogisticated nitrous gas" of Joseph Priestley by Dr. Mitchell's theory of contagion. Humphry Davy could only have become aware of this in Davies Gilbert's library and this indeed was discussed in the book which had been written earlier by Thomas Beddoes and James Watt called *Factitious Airs*. Dr. Samuel Lathom Mitchell was then professor of chemistry at Columbia College in New York City, but he had been a fellow student of Thomas Beddoes at Edinburgh. In this theory of contagion he tried to prove that Joseph Priestley's nitrous oxide had the power to spread disease when breathed by animals. He claimed that even the tiniest quantities on the skin or in the lungs were enough to cause this disease to spread. Since Dr. Mitchell apparently had made no experiments, Davy's critical mind quickly disposed of these arguments.

Davy himself not only tried it on animals, but he dared to breath it himself! His own account was as follows:

The fallacy of this theory was soon demonstrated by a few coarse experiments made on small quantities of the gas procured from zinc and diluted nitrous acid. Wounds were exposed to its action, the bodies of animals were immersed in it without injury and I breathed it mingled in small quantities in common air without remarkable effects. An inability to procure it in sufficient quantities prevented me at the time from pursuing the experiments to any greater extent. I communicated an account of them to Dr. Beddoes.

CHAPTER FOUR

An Opportunity Develops

In 1798, when Humphry Davy's interest in science was developing, Dr. Thomas Beddoes was establishing a Pneumatic Institution at Clifton, a suburb of Bristol. Dr. Beddoes was well known to both of Humphry's new friends. Davies Gilbert had been a student of Dr. Beddoes' at Oxford, and Gregory Watt, a consumptive, had been put in Dr. Beddoes' care by his famous father James Watt.

Beddoes was a remarkable man. Born in 1760, he had gone to Pembroke College, Oxford, receiving his Bachelor of Arts degree in 1781. He studied medicine under Sheldon, and then went to the University of Edinburgh, returning to receive his Doctor of Medicine degree in 1786 at Oxford.

In 1787 Beddoes was appointed Lecturer in Chemistry at Oxford, and it is here that Davies Gilbert studied under him, beginning a friendship that was to last a lifetime. By 1790 Beddoes was attempting to combine his two great interests, medicine and chemistry. The result was the development of a new scientific field which might be called pneumatic medicine, or medicine in relation to gases. He traveled to Bristol with the idea of setting up a Pneumatic Institution which would be a combination laboratory and hospital. Here the study of gases would be made a part of the experimental investigation directed toward the treatment of diseases. Fortunately, Beddoes received financial support from wealthy, enthusiastic acquaintances and friends and, as he built his staff of physicians, instrument-makers, and researchers, he began to look for someone to be superintendent of his laboratory.

Beddoes' medical practice had grown exceedingly. Bristol actually was a spa center—or mineral-spring resort—to which many sufferers, the asthmatic and consumptive, traveled in the hope of being cured at the Hotwells. Beddoes, seeking relief for his patients who breathed with difficulty, turned to the "airs," which a few years previously had been unknown. They included oxygen, discovered independently by Joseph Priestley and the Swedish scientist Karl Wilhelm Scheele; carbon dioxide studied by Joseph Black; and hydrogen, found by Henry Cavendish. Nitrogen had also been isolated. In addition, a very dangerous gas—hydrocarbonate, an impure carbon monoxide—was also known.

Beddoes prescribed inhalations of oxygen for many of his patients, especially those with shortness of breath.

The relief thus afforded the ailing encouraged Beddoes, and there developed an enthusiasm for it by the patients. However, his attempts to use impure carbon monoxide could have been highly tragic. Humphry Davy later almost killed himself breathing this poisonous gas. There is some suggestion, due to the inhalation of carbon dioxide by patients who then became drowsy, that Beddoes was close to the discovery of a form of anesthesia. Anesthesia was later to become the method for inducing unconsciousness in patients so that painless operations could be performed on them.

Early in 1798 Humphry Davy was enjoying the freedom of Davies Gilbert's library which included all of Beddoes' work. Here the young Davy, fresh from his recent beginnings in chemistry, found Beddoes' report of the contagion theory of Dr. Mitchell of Columbia. It was at this time that Davy was able to disprove the Mitchell theory, although his act of breathing the unknown gas to see the effects it might have on him was extremely dangerous. The fact that the gas had little effect upon Davy, of course, made Mitchell's theory absurd.

When Beddoes asked his friends to suggest names for the superintendent he was seeking for his institution, Davies Gilbert recommended Humphry Davy. Besides the work on nitrous oxide which Davy had sent him, Beddoes had also obtained Davy's theory on heat and light which Gregory Watt had forwarded.

Despite Davy's youth and relative inexperience, Beddoes was enough impressed with Davy's potential genius to ask Gilbert to persuade the youth to consider taking the position. Although Humphry Davy was eager to accept the position, he was shrewd enough to see that he had a bargaining position. It took some while for Davies Gilbert as middleman to arrange terms satisfactory to both Beddoes and Davy.

Davy was still apprenticed to Dr. Borlase, but the doctor was generous in this respect. He handed Humphry his indentures, releasing him from all claims. He felt certain that the offer from Dr. Beddoes would enhance Davy's opportunity to achieve fame and fortune.

Thus, on October 2, 1798, Davy left Penzance. He had never been outside the county of Cornwall. Watching the familiar countryside rolling away behind the galloping horses, he eagerly looked forward to his exciting future.

Davies Gilbert met him on the way to Bristol and they breakfasted together while Gilbert told him more of Beddoes and the Institution. As they ate, Davy's spirits were further aroused when the London mail coach rolled in covered with ribbons, bringing the news of Lord Nelson's victory of the Nile. He cheered with the others, and part of the cheering was for his own personal happiness.

CHAPTER FIVE

Early Days at the Pneumatic Institution

Bristol was the second largest city in England in 1798. To Davy it must have appeared a vast metropolis indeed. Although the once brisk trade that had brought ships from America, Africa, and Asia up the Bristol Channel and into the Avon River was now declining, the city was still regarded as the western capital of England.

Many famous English people of the day came to Bristol and were frequent guests in the great house in Rodney Place where Dr. Beddoes and his wife lived. Davy found Mrs. Beddoes a particularly agreeable and cultured lady. Since the young man was to stay with them until the Pneumatic Institution was established early in 1799, he found himself in the complete social whirl of the Beddoeses' house.

He wrote the following to his mother on October 11, 1798, only six days after his arrival, and his joy is very apparent: "I suppose you received my letter, written in a great hurry last Sunday, informing you of my safe arrival, and kind reception. I must now give you a more particular account of Clifton, the place of my residence, and of my new friends, Dr. and Mrs. Beddoes, and their family.

"Clifton is situated on the top of a hill, commanding a view of Bristol and its neighborhood, conveniently elevated above the dirt and noise of the city. Here are houses, rocks, woods, town, and country, in one small spot; and beneath us, the sweetly flowing Avon, so celebrated by the poets. Indeed, there can hardly be a more beautiful spot: it almost rivals Penzance, and the beauties of Mounts Bay.

"Our house is capacious and handsome; my rooms are very large, nice, and convenient; and, above all, I have an excellent laboratory. Now for the inhabitants, and first, Dr. Beddoes, who, between you and me, is one of the most original men I ever met—uncommonly short and fat, with little elegance of manners, and nothing characteristic externally of genius or science; extremely silent, and in a few words, a very bad companion. His behavior to me, however, has been particularly handsome. He has paid me the highest compliments on my discoveries, and has, in fact, become a convert to my theory, which I little expected. He has given up to me the whole of the business of the Pneumatic Hospital, and has sent to the editor of the *Monthly Magazine* a letter, to be published in November, in which I have the honor to be mentioned in the highest terms. Mrs. Beddoes is the reverse of Dr. Beddoes—extremely cheerful, gay, and witty; she is one of the most pleasing women I ever met with. With a cultivated understanding, and an excellent heart, she combines an uncommon simplicity of manners. We are already very great friends. She has taken me to see all the fine scenery about Clifton; for the Doctor, from his occupations and his bulk, is unable to walk much. In the house are two sons, and a daughter of Mr. Lambton, very fine children, from five to thirteen years of age.

"I have visited Mr. Hare, one of the principal subscribers to the Pneumatic Hospital, who treated me with great politeness. I am now very much engaged in considering of the erection of the Pneumatic Hospital, and the mode of conducting it. I shall go down to Birmingham to see Mr. Watt and Mr. Keir in about a fortnight, where I shall probably remain a week or ten days; but before then you will again hear from me. We are just going to print at Cottle's, in Bristol, so that my time will be much taken up, the ensuing fortnight, in preparations for the press. The theater for lecturing is not yet open; but, if I can get a large room in Bristol, and subscribers, I intend to give a course of chemical lectures, as Dr. Beddoes seems much to wish it.

"My journey up was uncommonly pleasant; I had the good fortune to travel all the way with acquaintances. I came into Exeter in a most joyful time, the celebration of Nelson's victory."

Among the frequent visitors to the Beddoeses' house were the poets Southey, Coleridge, and Wordsworth; the engineer James Watt; the Wedgwoods, whose fine china we know today; Maria Edgeworth, the famous novelist who was the sister of Mrs. Beddoes; Peter Roget who later developed Roget's *Thesaurus of English Words and Phrases,* and many others who brought the art of conversation, brilliant and witty, to the impressionable nineteen-year-old Humphry Davy.

Humphry Davy industriously threw himself into the work of the Pneumatic Institution. Two large houses had been leased and much laboratory apparatus was installed. This included the latest pneumatic equipment developed by the firm of Boulton and Watt.

On March 21, 1799, the new Medical Institute officially opened offering to treat patients free of charge. Great excitement prevailed. Surgeons and physicians connected with the Institute expected not only to treat patients but to do physiological experimentation with gases as well.

Meanwhile Davy had been exceedingly busy. Urged on by Dr. Beddoes, Davy was hurrying his speculations and experiments on heat and light for publication. At this time the young Davy, flattered by Dr. Beddoes' interest, could not see that his ideas had been accepted too readily. He did not yet understand that the critical attitude is of great assistance in the early development of hypotheses. Instead, in January, 1799, when Humphry Davy had just become twenty years old, these boyish notions were rushed into print.

In a volume called *Contributions to Physical and Medical Knowledge, Principally from the West of England,* collected by Thomas Beddoes, M.D., Humphry Davy's ideas were exposed to the critical view of British scientists. The first half of the book was given over to Humphry's essays and, in the remaining two hundred pages, Beddoes endorsed and praised Davy's ideas and even adopted the new names which Humphry had proposed to replace the ones used by Lavoisier.

The critics were quick to find fault with Humphry's overstatements, the conclusions which did not follow from experiment, and the general overenthusiasm of Humphry's approach. In fact, they tore his theory to pieces, shattering the young man's speculations.

As for Humphry Davy, he was ashamed and humiliated. He now began to realize that his hasty publishing of his "infant ideas" was a mistake. And if it was indeed a blunder, whose fault was it? Beddoes was an established man in the field. Humphry Davy was still a boy, who had begun to study science less than a year before and, while he may have been original in many of his ideas, he was also rash. Yet, instead of critical help, Humphry had received only praise and complete acceptance of his views. Since he had expected a man of sci-

35

ence like Beddoes to help him in the development of his career, praise from this man could only have made him feel that his own brilliance was assured.

Such acceptance would have turned any young man's head. In his letter to his mother (already quoted), he had been gleeful over Dr. Beddoes' conversion to his theory. Understandably, then, Humphry was very disturbed by the reaction to his views. For the rest of his life he was to wince at any mention of Beddoes' book. Long after he became famous, he expressed the view that he would gladly relinquish *whatever* glory and reputation he had since received if it were only possible to erase those essays.

Humphry did not regard the criticisms as being unjust. In August of 1799 he wrote manfully: "I was perhaps wrong in publishing in such haste. My mind was enthusiastic. Since that time, my knowledge of facts is increased; since that time I have become more skeptical."

In February of 1800 he even printed a public retraction of his theories in Nicholson's journal. It is possible that Humphry's relations with Dr. Beddoes had begun to cool before the publication of the essays. Humphry found the short, fat, silent Beddoes a very unsatisfying companion. Humphry liked to talk, to visit, to walk, to experiment. He later said of Dr. Beddoes as a teacher, "He was as unfit for a mentor as a weathervane is for a compass."

But the social life which Humphry found in Bristol was very exciting. "Mrs. Beddoes," he wrote, "is young, gay, and exceedingly popular. Not only does she enjoy walking and visiting places of interest, but she has many stimulating friends. The Beddoeses' home is a gathering place for poets and writers. Mrs. Beddoes' sister, Maria Edgeworth, already a famous novelist, is often here. The evenings I have spent with Robert Southey and Samuel Coleridge and with John Tobin the playwright have widened my world."

Humphry's own interest in stories, poetry, and conversation was stimulated by these celebrated visitors. Davy dreamed and planned of great writing projects of his own. Some of his poetry was published by Coleridge and Wordsworth in their annual anthology.

But these distractions did not keep him from chemistry. The disappointment which he had felt after the criticism of his essays only served to push him into further research. Already exciting possibilities were on the horizon. For Davy was again experimenting with "laughing gas."

CHAPTER SIX

Experiments with "Laughing Gas"

By April of 1799 Humphry Davy had already succeeded in obtaining nitrous oxide (N_2O, or "laughing gas") in a pure state. He had studied its chemical properties and decided to breathe it himself in its pure form. As we know, back in Penzance he had breathed in a little of this gas mixed with air, in the experiments which first attracted Dr. Beddoes. At that time he had noted no reaction.

On April 10, 1799, he wrote to his friend Davies Gilbert:

I breathed some pure nitrous oxide today in the presence of Dr. Beddoes and some others, sixteen quarts of it for seven minutes. It appears to support life longer than even oxygen gas, and absolutely intoxicated me. . . . It raised my pulse upwards of twenty strokes and made me dance about the laboratory as a madman and has kept my spirits in a glow ever since.

In other reports Davy describes the strange experience due to the effects of nitrous oxide: "My visible impressions were dazzling and apparently magnified; I heard distinctly every sound in the room." It was as if the stimulation from breathing nitrous oxide sharpened the senses as well as raised the spirits.

Of course, Davy's senses had been exceedingly sharpened by the criticism his heat and light experiments had received. He had warned himself in his notebook to "avoid the dangers of false generalization." Davy also realized the difficulty of forming true generalizations, and wrote: ". . . when I consider the variety of theories that may be formed on the slender foundation of one or two facts. . . ." How he must have winced!

Yet Davy had learned a great deal from his experience. He was cautious in making claims for the experiments which were presently being performed. There were now over eighty patients being treated in the hospital and many of them were receiving treatment with gases.

Beddoes had become convinced that most diseases could be treated by varying the proportion of oxygen breathed, or by using such other gases as nitrous oxide, hydrogen, or nitrogen, or gases obtained from the burning of vegetable or animal matter. Beddoes had already determined that inflammatory diseases were curable by lowered oxygen content, and that increased oxygen was useful for nervous patients or those suffering from "increased or diminished action of the arterial system."

As soon as Humphry Davy began his amazing series of researches with nitrous oxide, Beddoes wrote to his friend Erasmus Darwin * to say that phenomenal investigations were going on at the Pneumatic Institution. In fact, he believed that they were on the verge of discovering a panacea for all ailments. Credulous and easily swayed, Beddoes saw a glorious future for his Institution and seized upon the possibilities of nitrous oxide as a cure-all.

This time Humphry Davy was more careful. He was doubtful about some of the patients who appeared to be cured after the administration of nitrous oxide. He had already seen what an exhilarating and exciting effect the gas could have on his experiments upon himself. He devised a system of using "blank" experiments, that is, treating some patients without nitrous oxide, but telling them that they were indeed getting the same gas other patients were talking about. He did not tell Dr. Beddoes of this, however. (This method is essentially the method used today to check the effect of medicines or drugs on individuals who report improvement.)

When one of Dr. Beddoes' paralytic patients was pronounced cured after fourteen visits to the Institution, the doctor became so excited that he would not wait for the publication date of his volume of *Contributions* but

* Erasmus Darwin (1731–1802) was an English scientist, poet, and physician. He was the grandfather of both Francis Galton, famous biologist, and Charles Darwin, who was to develop the modern idea of evolution.

wished to insert reports in the newspapers and to print circulars for distribution to doctors, hospitals, and universities.

Humphry Davy then confessed to Beddoes that he and the poet Samuel Coleridge, who had acted as an assistant with the patient, had given no nitrous oxide at all to the paralytic! At the same time, however, the evidence that nitrous oxide had a very remarkable physiological effect could not be denied. Davy himself had demonstrated to his friends that it was not deadly and they had observed the strange reactions he had displayed. They rushed to try it themselves. Samuel Coleridge, whose brilliant poem *Kubla Khan* was said to have been written under the influence of opium, tested the flavor of "Davy's gas."

Coleridge wrote of this experience:

The first time I inspired the nitrous oxide, I felt a highly pleasurable sensation of warmth over my whole frame, resembling that which I remember once to have experienced after returning from a walk in the snow into a warm room. The only motion which I felt inclined to make was that of laughing at those who were looking at me.

The second time I felt the same pleasurable sensation of warmth, but not, I think, in quite so great a degree. I wished to know what effect it would have on my impressions; I fixed my eye on some trees in the distance, but I did not find any other effect except that they became dimmer and dimmer, and looked at last as if I had seen them through tears.

Even the calm, unruffled Robert Southey, later to be poet laureate of England, succumbed to the excitement of nitrous oxide. This excitement can be observed in a letter to his brother:

Oh, Tom! Such gas has Davy discovered, the gaseous oxide! Oh Tom! I have had some; it made me laugh and tingle in every toe and fingertip. Davy has actually invented a new pleasure, for which language has no name. Oh Tom! I am going for more this evening; it makes one strong and so happy, so gloriously happy! Oh, excellent air bag! Tom, I am sure the air in heaven must be this wonder-working air of delight.

Meanwhile, Humphry Davy continued to develop his researches on nitrous oxide and to record them in a lengthy memoir which was published in the year 1800. He had visited London for the first time in December of 1799, the month he reached his twenty-first birthday, and he met many of his friends from the Bristol circle there. Returning to Bristol, he was fired with energy and determined to finish writing his researches. Davy varied his methods of preparing nitrous oxide and tested the resulting products under different conditions. He tried the gas on animals and insects, and watched its influence on patients with different diseases.

In July, 1800, the six-hundred-page treatise by Humphry Davy, Superintendent of the Medical Pneumatic Institution, appeared under the title, *Researches, Chem-*

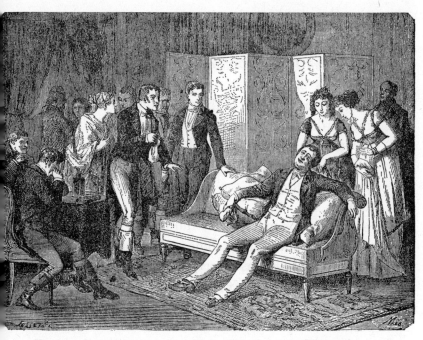

Humphry Davy experimenting with laughing gas at the Pneumatic Institution. (The Bettmann Archive)

ical and Philosophical; Chiefly Concerning Nitrous Oxide and Its Respiration.

In this book, which was to bring Davy immediate fame, he discussed all of the compounds of nitrogen then known, describing their properties and methods for their preparation. He also wrote of the preparation of nitrous oxide in enormous detail for use with patients, and exhaustively discussed the influence of the gas on living things.

The book is marvelously full of Davy's scientific approach. However, it has some faults. For example, Davy believed that air was a compound of nitrogen and oxygen rather than a mixture of gases, a misunderstanding, it appears, of Lavoisier's explanation of the composition of the air.

But in general his thoroughness is clearly displayed. In some cases, as in his comments on anesthesia, he was fifty years ahead of his time. Yet he failed to follow up the possibility of controlling physical pain with nitrous oxide, and thus painless surgery had to wait until 1844, when the American dentist Horace Wells demonstrated with an extraction of one of his own teeth that this was possible.

Humphry Davy himself had tried nitrous oxide while he was cutting one of his wisdom teeth. His gum was inflamed and he could not sleep due to the steady ache. Noticing that the pain diminished each time he had inhaled nitrous oxide, he wrote in his *Researches:*

Experiments with "Laughing Gas"

> As nitrous oxide in its extensive operation appears capable of destroying physical pain, it may probably be used with advantage during surgical operations in which no great effusion of blood takes place.

But apparently no doctor noticed the suggestion of pain suppression, so that anesthesia had to wait to be discovered. Davy meanwhile turned his attention to other gases and, in experimenting with them, almost killed himself.

CHAPTER SEVEN

Experiments with Other Gases

Today no scientist would take the risk of experimenting upon himself with a strange gas. Of course, we have a different view of gases. We know poison gases exist. The history of war, laboratory explosions, and newspaper accounts of chlorine, ammonia, and carbon monoxide poisonings are common knowledge.

But in Humphry Davy's time, "airs" were still seen as constituents of the atmosphere, and the ability of a particular gas mixture to sustain life—or not sustain it—depended on the proportion of "pure common air," or oxygen, it contained. That is, if animals died in an atmosphere of hydrogen, nitrogen, or carbon dioxide, it was regarded as due to the absence of oxygen. The physiological effect of nitrous oxide and its ability to burn were unique properties still little understood.

Since Humphry Davy had already been highly reinforced by the breathing of nitrous oxide, it was natural

46

that he would probably try further experiments with other gases. He had first attracted Beddoes' attention by slashing the Mitchell theory of contagion in a demonstration which ended in a damaging result to himself from breathing nitrous oxide, perhaps in impure form. Now, at the Pneumatic Institution, they were all using it in treatment and Davy had the enthusiastic cooperation of all his literary friends to vouch for the stimulating uplift to be obtained from "laughing gas."

Actually, from the results of "blank" experiments, Davy was already beginning to doubt that nitrous oxide had any lasting curative values. This naturally led him to wonder about the influence of other gases.

Although he spent much more of his time in the laboratory than in the hospital, Davy was aware of the medical work that the physicians of the Pneumatic Institution were undertaking. The many, many patients who flocked to the doors of the hospital, suffering from tuberculosis, asthma, and paralysis, came with either hope or desperation. Some of them had been given up as hopeless by their own doctors. Others had journeyed from far away to receive the benefits of the Bristol waters, but had not been helped. Many were dying. Thus, they looked to the Pneumatic Institution as a promise of delivery from pain and the threat of suffering and death.

As Davy's doubts about nitrous oxide increased, he felt this growing responsibility of the Institution toward

47

the patients. Beddoes urged Davy to increase his efforts in experimentation and so Davy sometimes found himself working twelve to fourteen hours a day.

Beddoes had noticed the influence which certain gases have upon animals. He had subjected kittens and rabbits to an atmosphere of oxygen and concluded that they had suffered. He observed that "kittens unconscious due to immersion in water recovered more quickly in oxygen than in air." He compared animals' reactions in oxygen with their reactions in hydrogen or in a carbon dioxide atmosphere. Actually, it is very unlikely that he was using pure gas, since the time factor reported in his data indicates considerable oxygen content for the animals to have survived as long as he claimed.

In his experiments with hydrocarbonate, Beddoes reported that animals were readily killed in this gas and remarked on the coloration of the blood of the dead animals. We know that the hydrocarbonate which he used was an impure form of carbon monoxide, a gas recognized today as very dangerous. Efforts to make airtight systems had fallen to James Watt, who proposed a sedan chair which would be two by three by five cubic feet and in which the patient could be restricted to an atmosphere of whatever gas was chosen for treatment, especially oxygen. This, of course, would have been a forerunner of today's oxygen tent.

Watt was very particular in his suggestions, and a tight room of eight or nine cubic feet had been proposed to Humphry Davy for experimenting with the hydrocarbonate gas. Watt cautioned Davy in the method of its preparation and in the method of its inhalation. Beddoes had observed that anemic patients derived special benefits from breathing the hydrocarbonate gas, for it caused the cheeks to color with a bright pink tinge. They were therefore anxious to use it since this appeared to bring such a look of health to the ailing patients. However, it did produce vertigo and dizziness in concentration, and it was for this reason that Watt repeatedly warned Humphry Davy about the method of administering the gas.

Davy had noticed with Beddoes that patients suffering from asthma appeared to be relieved after breathing oxygen, and had also observed that consumptives (tuberculars) had been able to go to sleep, without the use of opium, in an atmosphere deficient in oxygen. Beddoes had contaminated an atmosphere by adding nitrogen or hydrogen, and he knew that adding carbon dioxide induced drowsiness. He had used hydrocarbonate to induce sleep in consumptive patients.

At this point Humphry Davy was troubled about their inability to draw conclusions from patients' reports. We have already seen how he devised "blank" experiments in an effort to control this. He was puzzled over the change of symptoms in patients treated with gases, and perplexed at the proportions of the various gases used, as well as the difficulty of administering them. Moreover, he was suspicious of the purity of the gases themselves.

James Watt had been instrumental in devising the apparatus for the manufacture of the various gases and had written the full directions for the processes. Means of sealing joints, for example, had been described in detail. Despite this, however, the gases were manufactured from crude chemicals whose purity was not then measurable.

Davy went over the methods of the production of all these gases. Oxygen was produced from manganese oxide and, although washed with water, was still contaminated with some nitrogen. Nitrogen was obtained by drawing air over red-hot charcoal and the resulting gas being washed with limewater to take out the carbon dioxide. Carbon dioxide was obtained by the action of heat upon chalk or marble. The hydrocarbonate was produced by filling a fire tube with carefully prepared charcoal and, when red-hot, water was admitted. This resulted in a mixture of carbon monoxide and hydrogen much like the inflammable mixture we call "water gas" today.

Humphry Davy tried all the known gases in experiments upon himself. His notebooks contain detailed records of his sensations. In August of 1799 he tried breathing four quarts of hydrogen. He noted that his pulse grew feeble and his cheeks became purple. Needless to say, he stopped before he felt himself suffocating. Davy also noticed similar results with pure nitrogen. In the use of carbon dioxide, spasms prevented him from getting the pure gas into his lungs. Although he tried many times, it was not until he mixed the carbon dioxide with double the volume of air that he could manage to breathe it for nearly a minute. The only effect was a slight dizziness and a desire to sleep.

Although Davy knew of Beddoes' experiments in which animals had died from breathing hydrocarbonate, he went ahead and tried it himself. Moreover, he ignored Watt's warnings that this gas should be very much diluted to avoid the dizziness which it induced. This was what he wrote about the experiment:

> Having already inhaled for nearly a minute three quarts of hydrocarbonate mingled with nearly two quarts of atmospheric air, it produced a slight giddiness and pain in the head, and a momentary loss of voluntary power; my pulse was rendered much quicker and feebler. These effects, however, went off in five minutes, and I had no return of giddiness.
>
> Emboldened by this trial . . . I resolved to breathe pure hydrocarbonate. For this purpose, I introduced into a silk bag four quarts of gas nearly pure, which was carefully produced from the decomposition of water by charcoal an hour before, and had a strong and disagreeable smell.
>
> My friend, Mr. James Tobin, Jr., being present, after a forced exhaustion of my lungs, the nose being accurately closed, I made three inspirations and expirations of the

hydrocarbonate. The first inspiration produced a sort of numbness and loss of feeling in the chest, and about the pectoral muscles. After the second inspiration, I lost all power of perceiving external things, and had no distinct sensation, except a terrible oppression on the chest. During the third expiration, this feeling disappeared, I seemed sinking into annihilation, and had just power enough to drop the mouthpiece from my unclosed lips.

A short interval must have passed, during which I respired common air, before the objects around me were distinguishable. On recollecting myself, I faintly articulated, "I do not think I shall die." Putting my finger on the wrist, I found my pulse threadlike, and beating with excessive quickness. In less than a minute, I was able to walk, and the painful oppression on the chest directed me to the open air.

It is indeed a miracle that Davy did not kill himself. He was able to recover with the help of oxygen and nitrous oxide. Giddy and nauseated, he went to bed with a violent headache. While he was still weak the next day, he felt somewhat revived.

Yet so weakening had been the effects of this self-experimentation that Davy was obliged to return to Cornwall for a complete recovery. This probably saved his health from further injury and he resolved "never to perform so foolhardy an experiment again."

CHAPTER EIGHT

Davy's Early Electrical Experiments

Humphry Davy originally had come to Bristol with the intention of continuing his medical studies. Dr. Tonkin, whose hopes and care had meant so much to him, still had an influence upon Davy. Being an apprentice with the able Dr. Borlase, who had so kindly tutored him and so graciously released him from his indentures, had only stimulated his medical ambitions. Ultimately, Humphry Davy's aim was to go to the University of Edinburgh to become a qualified doctor of medicine.

One of the attractions for Davy in coming to the Pneumatic Institution was to work with the famous Dr. Beddoes, treating patients and studying illness and disease. Dr. Beddoes had written to Davies Gilbert, "This appointment will bear to be considered as a part of Mr. Davy's medical education." It was clear that medicine distinctly appeared to be Davy's future.

Yet Davy's position at the Institution required that a

great deal of his time be spent in the laboratory rather than in the hospital. Moreover, even when the opportunity to be in the hospital presented itself, Davy began to go less frequently. Perhaps he was somewhat repelled by the difficulties of diagnosis, the uncertainty of treatment, and the basic inability to do any real experimenting. Or perhaps, in the laboratory, he found that he could better control conditions of experimentation. Certainly he could choose his area of investigation. No constant conferences there. No threat of death, no suffering, no hopelessness of achieving some results. Furthermore, there was the possibility that out of the laboratory would emerge useful materials for treating or curing patients.

One of Davy's real interests in the laboratory centered on the materials and apparatus with which he could ask questions of nature, and then speculate about the answers to scientific problems from the results he got.

The laboratory at Hope Square was like the fulfillment of a dream. All the latest scientific apparatus for the study of gases that were available or that could be conceived by the shrewd mind of James Watt were here. As Davy looked at the large retorts, the "gasometers" for collecting gases, the breathing bags from Boulton and Watt, the shelves stacked with reagent bottles, glass instruments, and containers, he must have realized how far he had come from the homemade utensils of his early experiments as Dr. Borlase's assistant less than two years before.

Then a new experimental direction suddenly opened up! On April 30, 1800, the English scientists William Nicholson and Anthony Carlisle announced that water could be decomposed into its constituent elements, hydrogen and oxygen, by means of an electric current using a voltaic pile.

Humphry Davy was elated upon reading of this experiment. It would probably represent a plentiful source of pure hydrogen and oxygen! Then his thoughts leaped ahead. What was a voltaic pile? How could an electric current act like this? What did this separation of oxygen and hydrogen from water mean?

Davy knew very well that it had been the synthesis of hydrogen and oxygen to form water—achieved by Cavendish in 1781—that had cleared one of the last obstacles for Lavoisier's new theory of burning. James Watt had also been involved in that sequence of discoveries, as had Joseph Priestley. The hydrogen gas and the oxygen gas had been exploded by a spark, with water the only product.

But the voltaic pile was something new! Davy read anxiously to find out what this amazing thing was that Nicholson and Carlisle were using.

What he learned was that in 1791 a physician named Luigi Galvani in Bologna, Italy, described a remarkable observation in his laboratory. One of his assistants had been working with a partly dissected frog. In the same room another assistant was working with a machine that produced static electricity. As the second man drew a spark from the electrical machine, the assistant working with the frog accidentally touched the crural nerve of the frog's leg. The frog's leg gave a sudden twitch as if it were alive.

Galvani began to systematically investigate this accident. He noticed that the electrical machine was not really necessary. If the nerves in the frog's leg were merely touched by two different metals that were in contact, the leg of the dissected frog could be made to twitch. Galvani believed that he had discovered a living force which he called animal magnetism.

Alessandro Volta of the University of Pavia did not agree with Galvani's ideas on animal magnetism. Volta was a physicist and his experiments soon showed that whenever two different metals were made a part of an electric circuit, one of them showed a positive charge and the other a negative charge. He was able to publish a list of such metals in electro-potential order in 1792.

Volta began experimenting to get stronger electric currents and he found that with plates of zinc and copper, separated by pieces of cloth or paper soaked in salt solution, he could generate a fairly strong current. A report from Volta was sent to the Royal Society of London, and the President of this Society, Sir Joseph Banks, read it at a meeting in March, 1800.

By the end of April, Nicholson and Carlisle in England had reported on their accidental discovery that water could be decomposed into hydrogen and oxygen by the use of the voltaic pile.

Humphry Davy promptly repeated the experiments of Nicholson and Carlisle in his own laboratory at the Pneumatic Institution. By separating the positive and negative electrodes at some distance, he was able to collect and test for both gases. They were clearly hydrogen, the inflammable gas, and oxygen, the life supporter. What amazed Davy was the fact that no matter how far he separated the electrodes, the gas bubbles still arose at the same plates. He interposed his own body between the electrodes by holding the metal plates with either hand, and still the gases were generated.

Davy also noticed that if the water was pure there was no evolution of hydrogen and oxygen. No electric current flowed in pure water. He added a little caustic potash, and current immediately began flowing. He was startled that the caustic potash did not decompose at the electrodes. Davy still got only hydrogen and oxygen. If he added a little salt or a small amount of acid, the electric current could still be conducted and hydrogen and oxygen would be evolved. Even common air dissolved in the water permitted conduction for a brief period, and Davy was later able to demonstrate the impurities in air which made the conduction possible.

At the very beginning of this experimental work, Humphry Davy suspected an interchangeability between chemical and electrical energy. It was clear that electrical forces were bringing about a chemical change. And Davy, despite his promise to himself to be cautious, made the bold assertion that chemical forces could produce electricity. In 1800 he stated that the voltaic pile could only act if the electrolyte* reacted with the metal of the electrodes. The electrolyte had to be capable of oxidizing one of the metals of the electrode.

By the end of January, 1801, Humphry Davy had written six papers on the subject of the chemical changes which are involved when various substances are decomposed by an electric current.

Davy then came under the eye of the Royal Institution of Great Britain. It was more than his experiments with the electric current that made him attractive to the directors of the Royal Institution. At that time they were looking for someone to be the Director of the Laboratory and assistant lecturer in chemistry.

Professor Hope of the University of Edinburgh had learned of Davy from Dr. Beddoes and had read the work on nitrous oxide. Hope himself had gained fame by separating barium from strontium compounds many years before. He had met Humphry Davy during a trip to Bristol and had been very impressed with him. Davy knew a great deal about mineralogy and had himself collected some samples of strontium sulfate which he showed to Hope.

One of the founders of the Royal Institution, and probably the chief source of its beginning energy, was Count Rumford. Rumford, born in Massachusetts, in the United States, had gone to Prussia where he achieved enduring fame by his explanation of the nature

---

* A substance which when dissolved in a solvent (usually water) produces a conducting medium.

Davy experimenting with the decomposition of alkalies by means of the voltaic battery. (The Bettmann Archive)

of heat. When Hope proposed Humphry Davy to Count Rumford with such enthusiasm, it must have given Rumford cause to think of his own spirited rise in the scientific world. Moreover, Dr. Beddoes, in a publication, *On the Arrangement of Bodies According to Their Principles*, pointed out a simple experiment done by Humphry Davy on the nature of heat. Davy had melted two pieces of ice by rubbing them together! Of course, Rumford himself had shown how friction generates heat, and that heat is a form of energy rather than a material substance. Thus Rumford decided to interview Davy, not yet twenty-two years old.

CHAPTER NINE

Lecturer at the Royal Institution

In September of 1800, Humphry Davy had written to his mother to tell her that he believed his future prospects appeared brilliant. But it was not until the end of January, 1801, that he told anyone at home in any detail about his hopes. In this letter to his mother he said:

> You have perhaps heard of the Royal Philosophical Institution . . . Count Rumford has made proposals to me to settle myself there, with the present appointment of assistant lecturer on chemistry, and experimenter to the Institution; but this only to prepare the way for my being in a short time sole professor of chemistry, etc; an appointment as honorable as any scientific appointment in the kingdom, with an income of at least 500 pounds a year . . . Dr. Beddoes has honorably absolved me from all engagements at the Pneumatic Institution, provided I choose to quit it. However, I have views here which I am loath to leave, unless for very great advantages.
>
> You will, I dare say, be glad to see me getting amongst

the *Royalists,* but I will accept of no appointment except upon the terms of *independence.*

Davy made a trip to London in mid-February to arrange the details of his appointment to the Royal Institution. He took up residence there in March.

The Pneumatic Institution which Davy had left behind had seen its day. Pleasant though it was for him in the congenial atmosphere of the Bristol literary circle, sparked by the charm of Mrs. Beddoes, and great as were his opportunities to learn by working in his laboratory, Davy's decision to depart was a wise one. The Pneumatic Institution held no future for him. Patients chose not to be available for experiments, and the idea of the gases as cure-alls was hopelessly overambitious.

With Davy's fire and zest gone, the Pneumatic Institution limped on for only a little while. By 1803 a new organization called the Preventive Medical Institution was established, with a branch just outside the city, and Dr. Beddoes lived out a lifetime of rather pale contribution. Actually, the enduring contribution of the Pneumatic Institution had been Davy's work on nitrous oxide. As for Beddoes, his greatest triumph was clearly his launching of the scientific career of Humphry Davy.

Apparently Davy was not immediately successful in London. One report went that Count Rumford actually found the young Davy repulsive at first. Rumford was so disappointed in having engaged Davy that he refused to permit him to speak in the main theater until he had proved himself in the smaller lecture room.

On April 25, 1801, Humphry Davy delivered his first public lecture—in the small lecture room. Sir Joseph Banks, President of the Royal Society and Chairman of the Royal Institution, was present, along with Count Rumford. Present also were many distinguished scientists and philosophers. At first the ideals of the Royal Institution had attracted a wide following. Later, donations had fallen off, largely due to the unfortunate choice of lecturers, but there was still considerable scientific interest in the future of the Institution.

Davy's first lecture, however, was an unqualified success. Young as he was, his self-assurance was somehow coupled with a modesty of manner. His lecture was on the history of galvanism, and his knowledge of electricity was clearly reflected in his words and demonstrations.

The following account of Davy's lecture was published in the *Philosophical Magazine:*

> It must give pleasure to our readers to learn that this new and useful Institution, the object of which is the application of science to the common purposes of life, may be now considered as settled on a firm bases. . . .
>
> We have also to notice a course of lectures, just commenced at the Institution, on a new branch of philosophy—we mean the Galvanic Phenomena. On this interesting branch Mr. Davy (late of Bristol) gave the first lecture on the 25th of April. He began with the history of galvanism, detailed the successive discoveries, and de-

scribed the different methods of accumulating galvanic influence . . . He showed the effects of galvanism on the legs of frogs, and exhibited some interesting experiments on the galvanic effect of the solutions of metals in acids. . . .

Sir Joseph Banks, Count Rumford, and other distinguished philosophers were present. The members of the audience were highly gratified, and testified to their satisfaction by general applause. Mr. Davy, who appears to be very young, acquitted himself admirably well; from the sparkling intelligence of his eye, his animated manner, we have no doubt of his attaining a distinguished eminence.

The managers of the Institution promptly resolved to appoint Davy lecturer in chemistry, and Count Rumford at once promoted him to the "great theater" and ordered that the Royal Institution put everything it had at Humphry Davy's disposal.

Humphry Davy's lectures soon created a sensation. All kinds of people were attracted to them, from the ladies who sighed that "those eyes were made for something more than poring over crucibles," to the scientists who heard him discourse on recent ideas and discoveries in science. The literary circles led by his poet friends, such as Coleridge, also came to hear him.

The managers of the Institution then resolved "that a course of lectures on the Chemical Principles of the Art of Tanning be given by Mr. Davy" and he was sent out during the months of July, August, and September to acquaint himself with the business of tanning.

Davy returned to London at the end of September to work hard at galvanic experiments and to report on some of his chemical experiments on tanning. It is said that by his earnestness, knowledge, and eloquence he was even able to interest an audience on the tanning industry. But it was not until January 21, 1802, that Davy struck a thunderclap into the social and intellectual life of London. On that day he gave the first of his regular series of lectures.

Strangely enough, the prospects of the Royal Institution had fallen considerably during the autumn and early winter. The enthusiasm with which the project had been launched had faded beyond quick recovery. Count Rumford had managed the Institution in an overbearing manner and many powerful friends of science had withdrawn their support. The subscriptions had fallen from eleven thousand pounds to less than three thousand. It was Rumford himself who, in 1796, had started a Society for Bettering the Condition of the Poor, and the Royal Institution was partly an outgrowth of this Society. Sincere idealists who had expected that the Institution was to benefit humanity by its approach not only became doubters but some became outspoken enemies of Rumford.

Practical editorial writers predicted that this enterprise was to suffer the fate of all such ambitious projects part of whose aim was to help mankind. Yet the subject of Davy's lecture was to be on the value of science in the improvement of society. Accordingly, Rumford and the Institution managers launched a campaign to draw British scientists and philosophers to the lecture by spreading the word about Davy's abilities as a speaker. They wrote to their European colleagues and some came from other countries. The poet Samuel Coleridge passed the word among his literary friends. Dr. Beddoes' influence with a large politico-social group, the Tepidarians, resulted in the arranging of their festival to coincide with Davy's lecture, which they attended as a group.

For this powerful audience—political, social, literary, scientific, intellectual—Davy prepared a lecture designed to make science of interest to everyone. He had been busy for weeks in its preparation.

At last, on January 21, 1802, Humphry Davy faced a large, varied, and expectant audience.

He did not disappoint them.

With passionate enthusiasm, Davy outlined the services of science to mankind. He painted a picture of the moral and educational force science could be. He dwelt upon the contribution of scientists to the development of knowledge. He stated that men could look forward to a human progress aided by the learning of science which would arise out of the present. "We look for a time that we may reasonably expect," he concluded, "for a bright day, of which we already behold the dawn."

Davy's lecture was an astounding success, as the following contemporary account shows:

> The sensation created by his course of lectures at the Institution, and the enthusiastic admiration which they obtained, is at this period scarcely to be imagined. Men of the first rank and talent, the literary and the scientific, the practical and the theoretical, Bluestockings and women of fashion, the old and the young, all crowded—eagerly crowded—the lecture room. His youth, his simplicity, his natural eloquence, his chemical knowledge, his happy illustrations, and well-conducted experiments excited universal attention and unbounded applause. Compliments, invitations, and presents were showered upon him in abundance from all quarters; his society was courted by all, and all appeared proud of his acquaintance.

Humphry Davy was not prepared for the role of the social lion which he now became, but he adapted admirably. He was invited everywhere by leaders of fashion. Dinners and parties were hardly considered complete without him. For the twenty-three-year-old Davy, it had been a mighty jump from the modest homes of Penzance to the finest homes in London.

The future of the Royal Institution had now become assured. Moreover, Count Rumford became less and less its moving spirit. Rumford still had duties to the Elector of Bavaria, and his recent marriage to the widow of the French scientist Antoine Lavoisier had not turned out well. By 1803 he was no longer active in the affairs of the Institution. In addition, Sir Joseph Banks ceased his major activities soon afterward.

Thus the directing power that emerged was the energetic Humphry Davy.

CHAPTER TEN

Fellow of the Royal Society

Despite Humphry Davy's newfound success, he did not forget his family and his friends. His mother and sisters in Penzance received regular news, and he wrote frequently to his friends at Bristol and Penzance, and to others outside of London.

Although Davy appeared with increasing frequency as the honored guest at receptions and banquets, his notebooks grew crammed with experimental data and projected experiments he amassed over this period.

In May, 1802, Davy was elected professor of chemistry of the Royal Institution and, the following year, he was elected a Fellow of the Royal Society of London— one of the very few men not yet twenty-five years old who could write F.R.S. after his name. He was well on his way to becoming the "first scientist of his age."

Davy was not unaware of his good fortune in his lecture courses. He perceived, moreover, that his efforts were bringing an interest in science to people not ordinarily attracted to it. In a letter to Davies Gilbert he wrote:

> My labors in the Theater of the Royal Institution have been more successful than I could have hoped from the nature of them. In lectures, the effect produced upon the mind is generally transitory; for the most part, they amuse rather than instruct, and stimulate to enquiry rather than give information. My audience has often amounted to four and five hundred, and upwards; and amongst them some promise to become permanently attached to chemistry. This science is much the fashion of the day.

Thus it is clear that Davy was not deluded into thinking he spoke only to scientists.

Dr. John Davy has described that, in his efforts to assure success, Humphry Davy took great pains in preparing his lectures. "He was always in earnest," John Davy points out, "and although he often amused his audience, his first object was always to instruct, and what he wished as instruction was less the actual experiments which he demonstrated so well than the maintaining of the importance and dignity of science with a hope to kindling a taste for scientific pursuits."

The scholar Dr. Paris, often very critical of Davy, wrote:

> In the morning, he was the sage interpreter of nature's laws; in the evening, he sparkled in the galaxy of

fashion . . . but Davy on returning to his morning labors, never found that the thread had been unspun during the interruption.

For the next twelve years Humphry Davy was to occupy the chair of chemistry at the Royal Institution. His reputation as the greatest living lecturer on chemistry grew in that theater into which eager and fascinated audiences crowded. It was not merely Davy's art and his skill as a speaker that brought about this increasing success. The work he was developing in the laboratories was to bring an even greater fame to the Institution, for the published work which grew out of these experiments and lectures would long outlive the brilliant lectures Davy delivered.

The electrical experiments of Nicholson and Carlisle, which had so excited Davy while he was at the Pneumatic Institution, had been performed at the Royal Institution. The laboratory was well equipped for its time. It had been designed for research and contained a powerful blast furnace, iron forge, blowpipe, pneumatic and galvanic troughs, as well as all the chemical apparatus and delicate laboratory instruments that a mind like Count Rumford's could think of.

Davy's first paper on galvanism, following the Nicholson-Carlisle experiment, had been read to the Royal Society in 1801. His present fame rested solely on his nitrous oxide experiments in Bristol and his popular

My dear Sir

Permit me
to introduce to you
General Bentham who
wishes for the pleasure
of your acquaintance.
I rejoice that
your Philosophical Institution
is making so rapid a
progress. I thank you very
much for making me
acquainted with Mr Bigge
I am my dear Sir
with the greatest esteem
Royal Ins. yours H. Davy

A note written by Humphry Davy in December of 1803.
Addressed to Mr. James Losh of the Philosophical Institution, it
introduces a certain General Bentham. (Facsimile courtesy of
The Burndy Library)

chemistry lectures. The first assignment given to Davy by the management had been to do some research in tanning, and in February, 1803, Davy read the results of his researches before the Institution. His election as a Fellow came in November of 1803.

It was in this same year, 1803, that Davy's course of lectures on the chemistry of agriculture was begun. Each year he delivered a talk on that subject until 1813, when the series was published in a single volume.

In 1805 Davy's investigations turned to geology and he made a series of specimen-gathering trips which took him throughout England, Scotland, Ireland, and Wales. Thus his lectures that year were upon geological subjects.

Despite all these enormous demands on his time and energy, Davy's interest in electricity continued and, bit by bit, his experiments began to unravel the fundamental laws of electrochemistry.

In this way, Davy's greatest scientific contribution began to emerge, for before 1806 no great scientific advancement could be ascribed to him. It was to be after this year that great discoveries would be credited to Humphry Davy's name.

CHAPTER ELEVEN

Studies in Electrochemistry

In his Bakerian lecture of 1806, Davy gave the results of his experiments on electricity. It was entitled "On Some Chemical Agencies of Electricity." There were nine sections, and they probed vigorously into the problems of chemistry and electricity.

At the time Davy had repeated the experiments of Nicholson and Carlisle, he had been intrigued to see hydrogen bubbling off at one electrode and oxygen bubbling off at the other. How could these gases originate from the same water when such a considerable distance separated them? During electrolysis, Davy tried increasing the distance between the electrodes and could observe no lessening of the bubbling. As we have seen, he even interposed his own body into the circuit and noted that the gases were still produced.

Yet when pure water was used, the voltaic pile could not act. It was not until some salt or acid or even impurities such as ordinary air were present in the water that conduction was possible. What was happening? When caustic potash was added to pure water conduction was excellent, but amazingly enough the caustic potash itself was not decomposed.

Many experimenters had now begun to observe the formation of acid or alkalies around the two electrodes during electrolysis. Chemists were arguing hotly that these substances came from the pure water. The dispute raged on, despite Davy's evidence that pure water was a nonconductor. The use of litmus showed no presence of acid or base when pure water was the only path in the closed circuit of the voltaic pile. Periods of twenty-four hours, and even longer, made no difference. But if a little salt were added to the water, conduction became apparent, bubbles began to appear at the electrodes, and litmus rapidly gave color changes.

By a series of convincing experiments, Davy demonstrated that only impurities in "pure water" made conduction possible. Dissolved air, the solvent action of water on the vessel walls, faulty purification of the water, all were demonstrated by Davy to explain the varying results of arguing chemists.

In the second section of his lecture, Davy demonstrated that no matter what the substance used, acid matter is collected in the water around the positive pole and alkaline matter around the negative pole. Substances from many areas were subjected to electrolysis.

When he used metallic solutions such as iron, tin, or zinc, metallic crystals were deposited at the negative electrodes with an excess of acid appearing in the cup with the positive electrodes.

In the remaining seven sections of his report, Davy examined in great depth the effect of reversing current at each electrode, whether the acids or alkalies are formed in transit between electrodes, the opposite states of electricity after electrolysis, and the possibility of "chemical affinity."

The publication of this brilliant paper created a scientific sensation at home and abroad. J. J. Berzelius, the great Swedish chemist, called it one of the most remarkable memoirs to enrich the theory of chemistry.

Also remarkable was the report of the French Institute. Napoleon Bonaparte, who was then First Consul, had announced the establishment of a medal for the best experiment which should be made on "galvanic fluid." A committee of this Institute which included such giants as Laplace, Coulomb, Biot, and Halle awarded the medal to Humphry Davy.

However, since France and England were at war at this time, there was a great deal of bad feeling between the countries. Many felt that Davy should not accept the award. But Davy himself took a more sensible view of the whole idea. He wrote:

Some people say I ought not to accept this prize, and

there have been foolish paragraphs in the papers to that effect; but if the two countries or governments are at war, the men of science are not. That indeed would be a civil war of the worst description. We should rather, through the instrumentality of men of science, soften the asperities of national hostility.

Some of Davy's ideas expressed in his lecture of November, 1806, are far ahead of his time. The following statement by Davy is suggestive of our enormous electro-chemical industrialization today, as in the production of soap:

> It is not improbable that the electrical decomposition of neutral salts in different cases may admit of economical uses. Such an arrangement, if erected upon an extensive scale, neutrosaline matter being employed in every series, would, there is every reason to believe, produce large quantities of acids and alkalies with very little trouble or expense.

Also, Davy had made another observation which would enable him to discover two new elements the following year. He noticed that man's increased use of power could be employed to undo the chemical forces of nature. He wrote:

> The new mode of analysis may lead us to the discovery of the *true* elements of bodies, if the materials acted on be employed in a certain state of concentration, and the

electricity be sufficiently exalted. For if the chemical union be of the nature which I have ventured to suppose, however strong the natural electrical energies of the elements of bodies may be, yet there is every probability of a limit to their strength: whereas the powers of our artificial instruments seem capable of indefinite increase.

The young man who now stood so high in the opinion of world scientists had most of his greatest discoveries still ahead of him.

Despite Davy's busy schedule, he still took time to travel whenever he could. There exists a report concerning Humphry Davy's boyish appearance at this time. In 1805 Davy had gone on a vacation to the Lake Country where he met Sir Walter Scott, who was in the company of Davy's own friend, the poet Wordsworth. He then traveled to Northern Ireland to study the geology of that region. Here he met the Bishop of Raphoe, whose young sister was later to become Lady Brownrigg. The young woman left this account of her meeting with Davy:

We had been invited (I say *we,* for I was then with the Bishop of Raphoe) by Dr. Richardson to go to his cottage at Portrush, "to meet the famous Mr. Davy." We arrived a short time before dinner. In passing through a room we saw a youth, as he appeared, who had come in from fishing, and who, with a little notebook, was seated in a window seat, having left a bag, rod, etc., on the ground. He was very intent upon this little book, and we

77

passed through unnoticed. We shook hands with our host and hostess, and prepared for dinner. I went into the drawing room, under some little awe of this great philosopher, annexing to such a character at least the idea of an elderly grave gentleman, not perhaps, with so large a wig as Dr. Parr, or so sententious a manner as Dr. Johnson—but certainly I never calculated on being introduced to the identical youth, with a little brown head, like a boy, that we had seen with his book, and who, when I came into the drawing room was in the most animated manner recounting an adventure on the Causeway which had entertained him and from his manner of telling it was causing loud laughter in the whole room.

During the summer of 1806 Davy again visited Ireland, but in 1807 new responsibilities kept him from traveling, except for a quick trip to Cornwall to see his relatives.

In that same year Davy was elected Secretary of the Royal Society. His cousin Edmund Davy was now working as his assistant in chemistry, and together they did some chemical experimentation. One of Humphry Davy's duties was to see the issues of *Philosophical Transactions* through the press. On September 12, 1807, he wrote to Davies Gilbert that he had been doing considerable work on distillation.

Near the end of September Davy, with the help of his assistant, resumed his experiments in electricity. Using the voltaic pile, he began to explore the electrical action on alkalies.

Davy's notebook indicates that he was not testing a hypothesis or attempting to solve any particular problem when he began to work with the solutions of caustic potash.* Instead, he was systematically trying alkalies under the voltaic action, and studying the results. What led him to move from water solutions to try the electric current on melted potash will probably never be known.

On October 6, 1807, Humphry Davy connected the electrodes to the molten liquid and his eyes widened with surprise and joy at what he saw.

* Potassium hydroxide.

CHAPTER TWELVE

Discovery of Potassium and Sodium

Humphry Davy had combined three voltaic batteries to send an electric current through fused potash. One battery had consisted of 24 plates of copper and zinc, twelve inches square, the second had 100 plates of six inches, and the third battery had 150 four-inch plates. As the minute globules of potassium reached the surface of the potash crust, they burst into fire.

Davy could not hold back his joy. "He bounded about the room in ecstatic delight," Edmund Davy reported later. It took a while before he could calm down long enough to consider the significance of what he was observing.

Davy realized that the brief metallic glint of the bubbles and their explosion into a lavender fire had to be subjected to a good deal of thought. Experiments that lead to other experiments sometimes suggest themselves in profusion. In an eager, questioning mind like Davy's, they triggered a flood of speculation.

Humphry now had about six weeks to go before November 19, 1807, on which date he was scheduled to give his second Bakerian lecture. Those weeks were the most intensively exciting of Davy's career. It is almost incredible that in the short time between the first observation and this, the most memorable of Davy's Bakerian lectures, he had developed a series of results which filled forty-four pages, almost every page of which reported new findings.

Critics have often stated that Davy was just lucky in his discovery of the metals of the alkalies, and that he was only able to isolate them because the Royal Institution placed at his disposal a large, powerful voltaic battery. One authority, T. E. Thorpe, has stated that this criticism is incorrect. It was actually a battery of moderate dimensions which Davy pieced together and it was only later, in 1809, that Davy's successes in electro-chemistry encouraged a subscription to finance the construction of a large battery.

Other critics have felt that there was luck, too, in Davy's happening to use molten potash instead of a water solution of materials such as other experimenters were using. But how many times in the history of science has it happened that an unusual or unexpected observation has led to a new experimental direction?

In Davy's case, how did he happen to melt down the potash which made his experiment possible? He had noticed that, when wet, the potash conducted readily, and he knew that potash in water solution conducted the electric current. He was still interested in the fact that oxygen and hydrogen were evolved at the two electrodes no matter what material was added to the water, and he was attempting to explore the concentrations which he could now detect forming around the electrodes.

Also, he noticed that potash which had become damp after being exposed to air could now conduct the electric current. When he tried this he observed that the potash "fused and decomposed." It was probably in following up this observation that Davy and his assistants did the experiment reported on October 6. Davy wrote:

> Under these circumstances a vivid action was soon observed to take place. The potash began to fuse at both its points of electrization. There was a violent effervescence at the upper surface; at the lower, or negative surface, there was no liberation of elastic fluid; but small globules having a high metallic luster, and being precisely similar in visible characters to quicksilver appeared, some of which burnt with explosion and bright flame, as soon as they were formed, and others remained, and were merely tarnished, and finally covered by a white film which formed on their surfaces.

Although he had used a "platine" wire, he quickly established that using platine was not essential, for copper, silver, gold, plumbago, or even charcoal gave the same result when they were used to complete the circuit.

After his discovery of the element potassium (derived

from the word "potash"), Davy immediately rushed into new experiments. A few days later he had evolved sodium,* the second new element he had discovered in these few days. Of course, Davy was still struggling with impurities, and it is very likely that much of his original potassium was alloyed with sodium. He tried to carefully determine and describe the properties of the new metals. However, he could not be certain that he had either potassium or sodium free of each other. Both substances when exposed to air lost their metallic luster immediately, and both were quickly reconverted into potash and soda, respectively, by absorption of oxygen and moisture.

Davy tried hard to preserve them but it was impossible in air, and most liquids did not help. In water they burst into fire. He was finally able to keep them in naphtha. In heating both metals in oxygen, Davy noted the brilliant white flames which resulted. He also noted their extraordinarily low specific gravity by comparing globules of the potassium metals with the weight of mercury. Davy found the specific gravity of sodium by flotation in a mixture of naphtha and oil of sassafras.

All this while Davy was debating with himself whether the elements he had discovered could really be called metals because of their very light weight. But in the end he concluded that luster, malleability, conduc-

---

* Cartwright reports that the name Davium was first proposed for potassium, but that Davy refused to accept it. Both sodium and potassium were named for the bases from which they were obtained.

tion of heat and electricity, and chemical combining power rendered them indeed metals. In the short period of six weeks, discoveries of immense magnitude were made and analyzed, and a report was drafted.

On November 19, 1807, he delivered his second Bakerian address. It was received with wild enthusiasm by an awestruck audience. In a brilliant performance Davy exhibited metals never before seen by mankind. If his first lecture had been a masterpiece, his second was even more so.

But Davy's great triumph was costly.

Working at high pitch, Davy, in his excitement, ignored a developing fever. Shortly after his lecture he collapsed. As it turned out, the illness proved to be nearly fatal. The sickness was probably typhus and Davy himself thought he had contracted it from prisons, particularly Newgate, which he had been visiting so that he might suggest means of fumigating and disinfecting the huge buildings. John Davy, however, wrote that his brother's doctors attributed his illness to overfatigue. At any rate, Davy was put to bed on November 23, and nine weeks later he was still convalescing.

It is curious that so great was Humphry Davy's popularity that his bout with death only added to his fame. The flood of inquiries to the Royal Institution was such that the authorities put out bulletins regarding his condition four times a day.

Because of Davy's illness, the Royal Institution was

Davy conducting an experiment before the Royal Society.
(Courtesy of The Burndy Library)

obliged to obtain another speaker to open the 1808 session, and Dr. Dibdin chose to make an address regarding Humphry Davy:

> Mr. Davy, whose frequent and powerful addresses from this place, supported by his ingenious experiments, have been so long and so well known to you, has for these last five weeks been struggling between life and death. The effects of those experiments recently made in illustration of his late splendid discovery, added to consequent bodily weakness, brought on a fever so violent as to threaten the extinction of life. Over him it might emphatically be said, in the language of our immortal Milton, that
>
> > . . . *Death his dart*
> > *Shook, but delayed to strike.*
>
> His illness, severe as it has been, is now, however, beginning to abate, and we may reasonably hope, from present appearances, at least, that the period of convalescence is not very remote.

However, this hope was nip and tuck. Davy actually was severely ill, and had it not been for the day-and-night attention of his nurse and his cousin Edmund, he might well have been lost.

Yet by spring he was sufficiently recovered to report with dismay that, while he had been ill, other chemists such as Berzelius and Gay-Lussac had gotten ahead of him.

Chlorine and Its Compounds

Having now regained his health, Humphry Davy eagerly went back to his experimentation. During his convalescence, a voltaic battery of 600 plates, four times as powerful as any before constructed, had been installed. (A 2,000-plate battery was not constructed until the following year.)

Gay-Lussac, Thénard, and other French chemists had found a way of producing larger quantities of potassium than Davy's method produced. Also, Berzelius, the great Swedish chemist, had used a variation of Davy's process to isolate calcium and barium.

Using Berzelius' ideas, Davy now succeeded in isolating magnesium and strontium. He also obtained pure calcium and barium by distillation, and later succeeded in isolating the element boron.

In his overeagerness to publish and thus stake his strong claims for being first, Davy hurried his work. The

87

result of his hastiness was that his Bakerian lecture of 1808 was a general disappointment. Again in 1809, though his conclusions about tellurium are significant, Davy's work on hydrogen is made difficult by his own belief that hydrogen was a compound.

Now, behind his back, word began to go around that Davy was through. He had seen his zenith. The great days of his discoveries of nitrous oxide and potassium had been first-magnitude triumphs—how could one expect such efforts to be equaled?

At this time, too, the thirty-year-old Humphry Davy was in a great social whirl. Dr. Paris, in his biography of Davy, wrote that the scientist had so many appointments that he would dash out of his rooms at the Institution wearing five shirts, removing one after each visit.

In 1810, however, Humphry Davy began some of his greatest work—a systematic study of chlorine.

During this period, French and English chemists were engaged in great rivalry, and competition was keen. Davy, anxious for fame, fed his own vanity. But he was also aware that the quality of his work had fallen off. For example, he had found himself writing appendixes and doing supplementary experiments to make his last two Bakerian lectures more clear—yet this had only served to add to their confusion.

What it was that initially drew Davy's attention to chlorine we do not know, but it is possible that his jealous eye on the French chemists led him to investigate the controversy then raging about this gaseous material.

Karl Wilhelm Scheele, a Swedish chemist, had discovered chlorine in 1774. Scheele was a believer in the phlogiston theory of that time. Born in Pomerania in 1742, he had been apprenticed to a druggist, from whom he learned chemistry. A tireless investigator, Scheele managed to perform a vast amount of brilliant experimental work under the most adverse of conditions. But the exhausting night hours he kept, his work with very poisonous materials, and his tendency to taste and smell the chemicals he worked with probably brought on his early death at the age of forty-three, in 1786. Because of his chemical beliefs, Scheele named the greenish-yellow gas he had discovered "dephlogisticated marine air."

On the other hand, the great French chemist Antoine Lavoisier believed that oxygen occurred in all acids, and he named what we now call chlorine "oxymuriatic acid."

It is likely that Davy saw his chance to resolve the doubt about chlorine. As it happened, both of the above ideas contained errors and Davy's work demonstrated this. Yet he concluded that Scheele was the more correct of the two men.

On July 12, 1810, Davy read his paper on chlorine before the Royal Society, and it has been described as one of his most brilliant productions. In it, he compared the chemical notions of Scheele and the French school, concluding that:

It is evident from this series of observations that Scheele's view (though obscured by terms derived from a vague and unfounded general theory) of the nature of the oxymuriatic and muriatic acids may be considered as an expression of facts; whilst the view adopted by the French school of chemistry, and which, till it is minutely examined, appears so beautiful and satisfactory, rests in the present state of our knowledge upon hypothetical grounds.

John Davy's account is particularly interesting for he, too, had begun to work in the field of chemistry. Twelve years younger than his brother Humphry, he was now only nineteen years old. His work in Hope's laboratory in Edinburgh clearly demonstrated that chlorine contained no oxygen.

On November 15, 1810, Humphry Davy gave his fifth Bakerian lecture. He reported that he had extended his experiments with chlorine, and he discussed many of its compounds. He had, he said, observed that the bleaching effect of chlorine was due to its ability to decompose water so that oxygen was liberated.

Although Davy's experiments appeared to denounce completely the French view, that view still persisted. A controversy continued to rage in which Berzelius, Scheele's countryman, was the foremost defender of oxymuriatic acid. But eventually even Berzelius gave in and admitted his weak ground by reportedly telling his cook, "Thou must call it *chlorine,* Anna." This wide discussion brought about much investigative activity in chemistry and, as so often happens, led to fresh discoveries in the field.

Oddly enough, in this fifth Bakerian lecture, Davy chose to attack the respected English chemist John Dalton. One biographer observes that it was an unnecessary attack and displayed "a characteristic exhibition of temper." John Davy says nothing of his brother's attack upon Dalton. At any rate, there seems to have been a reason behind it.

Born in 1766, John Dalton was twelve years older than Humphry Davy. A poor boy, he worked as a farm laborer, and taught in the Quaker school at Eaglesfield when he was only twelve years old. He was appointed a teacher of mathematics and natural philosophy at the New College, later to become Manchester College, Oxford. In 1803, he published his paper "Absorption of Gases by Water and Other Liquids" in which his law of partial pressures occurs. Gradually his ideas began working toward the atomic theory for which he is best known and, by 1808, he published his views in his "New System of Chemical Philosophy."

Dalton had given a course of lectures at the Royal Institution in 1804 and delivered another course in 1809–10. Yet he was not to be made a Fellow of the Royal Society until 1822, when he was fifty-six years old.

There are two possible reasons for Davy's attack on Dalton and the atomic theory. First, Davy had been stung by overtheorizing when he permitted Dr. Beddoes to publish his "infant chemical speculations," exposing him to what he regarded as merciless criticism. While Davy himself was an experimenter, history has clearly demonstrated that Dalton was not. Although Davy could accept the law of definite proportions, he regarded Dalton's speculations from this law as spurious.

The second possible reason is simply that Davy was jealous of Dalton's developing stature. The vanity in Davy's nature demanded that he himself be supreme.

Yet people of very different personalities become scientists. As for the gentlemanly John Dalton when asked what he thought of the brash young Davy who had attacked him, he replied simply, "He is a very agreeable and intelligent young man."

CHAPTER FOURTEEN

Courtship and Marriage

Late in the year of 1811, Humphry Davy became aware of a brilliant star in London's night life. Her name was Jane Apreece. A highly popular young woman, she was often the center of attention in groups where Davy himself was accustomed to being in the spotlight. It was clear that the admiring male glances thrown in her direction indicated her universal attraction.

"Who is that brunet of the brunets?" Davy asked, fascinated.

Jane Apreece was a widow. Her father was Charles Kerr, a plantation owner, who had vast sugar holdings in Antigua in the West Indies. She was also a cousin of the great novelist Sir Walter Scott. Davy was elated to learn this, for he had a great admiration for Scott; and, of course, he regarded himself as one of the literary class. Jane Apreece had been one of the leaders of Edinburgh society—"a lioness of the first magnitude."

One of Davy's friends noticed his interest. He jostled Davy's elbow.

"You have many rivals," he said.

Davy straightened, turned his head, and cocked his eyebrow. The spirit that made him a champion in field and stream and which made him a whirlwind in the laboratory swept him with confidence. There was no doubt in his mind but that he would outrun any rivals.

"She is a very wealthy young widow," others told him.

Soon Humphry Davy fell deeply in love with Jane Apreece. It must have been a curious romance. While he was showering her with love letters, he was also burning the midnight oil at a strenuous rate, attempting to finish the longest work he ever produced. This was his *Elements of Chemical Philosophy,* a work which was intended to span the whole scope of chemistry.* At the same time he was compiling his *Elements of Agricultural Chemistry,* a work which brought together the lectures which he had been giving annually since he had joined the Institution.

Jane Apreece found the magnetic Humphry Davy more than a little attractive. She also hit upon a clever way to gain his attention. She expressed a deep interest in fishing.

This, of course, delighted Davy. He offered to loan her his copy of Izaak Walton's *The Compleat Angler,*

---

* The work was published in June, 1812, and no subsequent volumes were written.

or the Contemplative Man's Recreation, which offer she eagerly accepted. In his enthusiasm and excitement, Davy forgot he had loaned his book to someone else. Thus he was obliged to write her the following note:

> Mr. Davy regrets that he cannot send Walton to Mrs. Apreece this morning. He did not recollect that he had lent the book to a friend who lives a little way out of town. He will send honest Izaak to Mrs. Apreece tomorrow or Thursday.
>
> Mrs. Apreece is already of the true faith of the genuine angler. . . .

On the other hand, Davy attempted to enjoy those pastimes which interested her. He wrote to her, with tongue in cheek, since he knew Jane Apreece's interest in opera: "I begin to like the opera from association. The same association would, I think, make me love a desert. . . ."

To Davy, the music must have been a jumble indeed, for his brother John revealed that Humphry was tone-deaf. In addition, John Davy wrote that Davy would scoot about the laboratory humming a number of weird refrains.

Humphry Davy, of course, represented quite a catch himself, for at this time he was at the peak of his fame. Also, he was far from being poverty-stricken. Yet the story still persists that Davy married Mrs. Apreece because of her wealth.

In 1810 the Royal Dublin Society invited Davy to deliver a series of lectures on electrochemistry at their new laboratory. He eagerly accepted the offer, for the Society offered four hundred guineas, which was more than his annual pay at the Royal Institution. Not only was the amount handsome for the short period involved, but Davy enjoyed fishing the Irish streams and hunting for geological specimens.

Previously, Davy had been considering either the clergy or continuing his medical studies as a means of securing his financial future. The Dublin offer fortunately erased any need to give these ideas further consideration at this time. His lectures in Dublin were a great triumph. In fact, the Royal Dublin Society was so pleased that it passed a resolution that Davy be "requested to accept the sum of *five* hundred guineas."

Davy's brother John was in a position to appreciate his success, for he had been living with Humphry for the three years up to 1811. John wrote that "He had earned an unsullied and noble reputation; he was loved and admired by friends, who had cheered him on in his career. . . ."

The Royal Institution now depended on him entirely. His popularity was at its highest. He had been asked again in 1811 to lecture for the Royal Dublin Society— this time for seven hundred and fifty guineas—and reports which flooded back from his lectures in Ireland added to his prestige.

As for Jane Apreece, Humphry Davy, on January 1, 1812, was writing to his "darling":

> I hope the cold weather has not increased your indisposition and that the foggy sky has not made you melancholy. I trust you are now well and happy; I give myself pleasure by believing that you are.
>
> I have a motive for writing this day besides that of doing what I like. I find that Friday the tenth is a Royal Society Club day and that I ought to dine with the Club. All other days are yours and *that* shall be yours if you command it, but I know you wish me to do what I *ought* to do, and you *now* cannot doubt the exclusive nature of your influence and the absolute nature of your power.

On April 8, 1812, Mr. Humphry Davy became Sir Humphry Davy. The Prince Regent conferred the honor of knighthood upon him. On April 9, 1812, Davy gave his farewell lecture as professor of chemistry at the Royal Institution. His lecture was on metals, and taking notes at the lecture was a serious young man by the name of Michael Faraday.

Four days later, on April 12, 1812, Sir Humphry Davy and Mrs. Jane Apreece were married. During that spring and summer they traveled to the north of England and to Scotland. The new Mrs. Davy expected that they would remain in Scotland until December, but in October a challenge had appeared exciting enough to send Davy rushing back to England.

CHAPTER FIFTEEN

A New Explosive Substance

Not even at the height of his romance with Mrs.
Apreece had Humphry Davy ceased working on his
scientific experiments. In fact, on all his travels—including his honeymoon—Davy carried along "his fishing
tackle and a portable chemistry chest." When he was
in Edinburgh he managed to visit his brother John in
his laboratory, and together they worked on some chemical experimentation. Humphry wrote the following to
his brother not long after his wedding:

> I communicated to you in a former letter, my plans, as
> they were matured. I have neither given up the Institu-
> tion, nor am I going to France; and wherever I am, I
> shall continue to labor in the cause of science with a zeal
> not diminished by increase of happiness and (with respect
> to the world) increased independence.
> I have just finished the first part of my "Chemistry" to
> my own satisfaction, and I am going to publish my "Agri-

cultural Lectures" for which I am to get 1,000 guineas
for the copyright and 50 guineas for each edition, which
seems a fair price. . . .

Also while he was in Scotland, Davy received a letter
from André Ampère, the French scientist for whom the
unit of current in electricity is named. Ampère told him
about a compound of chlorine and nitrogen which was
very explosive. The heat of one's hand was enough to
set it off. Dulong, the French scientist who had made
the discovery, had lost an eye and a finger in handling
it. Ampère had not given details but Davy excitedly
tried to manufacture the compound. He began with
ammonia at low temperatures combined with chlorine,
but this proved the wrong direction.

Davy still felt that nitrogen itself was a compound
and perhaps he hoped to prove it by an explosive series
of experiments which would break nitrogen down.
Nitrogen trichloride, the compound which Ampère had
described, is a yellow, very explosive oil. It is so unstable
that it can explode on exposure to bright light. Contact
with turpentine, heat, or shock can also set it off.

This was the situation in October when Davy returned to England, in order to have use of a full laboratory. He again began blending ammonia with
chlorine. It was only after many failures that Davy
succeeded in making the material by using an excess of
chlorine on ammonia. On that day, as he bent breath-

lessly over his materials, he saw the yellow oil beginning to form.

Then there was a blinding flash—it had exploded directly in his face! Although Davy tried to minimize the seriousness of his accident, it was critical enough to throw him out of action for many months, and to endanger the sight of one eye. Not until April of 1813 was Davy able to return to regular experimental work. As soon as he could, he went back to challenge the explosive nitrogen trichloride.

By June he had determined the specific gravity of the substance and he had learned many details concerning its nature. Nevertheless he was mistaken in believing its "formula" to be NCl_4. (Actually, the correct chemical notation for this substance is NCl_3.)

Upon his return to work in April, Davy also investigated another substance. He now attacked the chemistry of fluorine. The following is what he wrote his brother John on April 4, 1813:

I am now quite recovered, and Jane is very well, and we have both enjoyed the last month in London. I have been hard at work. I have expelled fluorine from fluate of lead, fluate of silver, and fluate of soda by chlorine. It is a new acidifier, forming three powerful acids; hydrofluoric, silicated fluoric, and fluoboric. It had the most intense energies of combination of any known body, instantly combining with all metals, and decomposing glass. Like the fabled waters of the Styx, it cannot be preserved, not even in the ape's hoof. We have now a triad of supporters of combustion.

The work on fluorine was read to the Royal Society on July 8, 1813. Davy pointed out in this paper that Ampère had made comparisons which had convinced him (Davy) of large similarities between chlorine and fluorine compounds. In addition, Davy's paper discussed silicon fluoride and hydrogen fluoride, both discovered by Scheele, although Gay-Lussac and Thénard were the first to obtain hydrofluoric acid in a pure state.

Davy then proceeded to describe his search for fluorine. In that search his experiments proved to be both chemical and electrochemical. At the end of his paper, Davy concluded that most of the compounds he had been investigating were of metals united with fluorine, a prediction that was later to be definitely verified.

With some important years still lying ahead of him, Humphry Davy had already made another great "discovery." But this one was quite outside the laboratory, and no one knew about it yet.

CHAPTER SIXTEEN

Davy's Greatest "Discovery"

A curious statement frequently made about Torben Olof Bergman, the famous Swedish physicist and chemist, is that his greatest discovery was a man—Karl Wilhelm Scheele. The same statement is often made about Humphry Davy. For despite his great scientific contributions, Davy's greatest "discovery," too, was a man. That man was Michael Faraday.

On September 22, 1791, at Newington Butts, London, Faraday was born in poor circumstances. His father was a blacksmith who had come from Yorkshire. By the time Michael Faraday was fourteen years old, his family had moved to North London. Young Michael was then apprenticed to a bookbinder and bookseller.

It was while serving this apprenticeship that Faraday learned to read. He would pore over the many books which were left in the shop. Particularly struck by the books about science, he devoured these with keen interest and excitement.

By 1812 Faraday's father had died and Michael aided his older brother in the care of his mother and sisters. Michael Faraday found that while his interests were wide, his future seemed hopeless. He was not happy in bookbinding and he could not see any future hope for himself in any of the trades.

One day a member of the Royal Institution, a Mr. Dance, came to the shop of Faraday's master to leave the sheets for some chemical works to be bound. So fascinated was young Faraday that he sat up all night reading the material, much of which he could retain since he had an excellent memory. When the works were not ready at the prescribed time, the angry and impatient Mr. Dance rushed over to the shop himself to find out what was holding up the delivery.

Mr. Dance was in for a surprise. He found the young bookbinder teaching himself chemistry. One story has it that Mr. Dance was so impressed that he suggested Faraday keep one of the books, and the book chosen was one by Humphry Davy.

"You know, he is the professor of chemistry at our Institution," Mr. Dance told him.

"Yes, I know."

"Have you been to one of his lectures?"

"Oh, no sir." Faraday dropped his hands. "It is too costly and I have no money that I could spare."

"Very well, young man," Mr. Dance announced. "To hear our Mr. Davy is an unforgettable experience. I shall take you to hear one of his lectures."

Mr. Dance kept his promise and the young book-binder was filled with awe at hearing the famous scientist speak.

Seventeen years later—after Humphry Davy's death —when Dr. Paris asked Michael Faraday to tell him about his first meeting with Davy, Faraday wrote this letter:

My Dear Sir,

You ask me to give you an account of my first introduction to Sir H. Davy, which I am very happy to do, as I think the circumstances will bear testimony to his goodness of heart.

When I was a bookseller's apprentice, I was very fond of experiment and very averse to trade. It happened that a gentleman, a member of the Royal Institution, took me to hear some of Sir H. Davy's last lectures in Albemarle Street. I took notes, and afterwards wrote them out more fairly in a quarto volume.

My desire to escape from trade, which I thought vicious and selfish, and to enter into the service of Science which I imagined made its pursuers amiable and liberal, induced me at last to take the bold and simple step of writing to Sir H. Davy, expressing my wishes, and a hope that, if an opportunity came in his way, he would favor my views; at the same time I sent the notes I had taken at his lectures.

The answer, which makes all the point of my communication, I send you in the original, requesting you to take great care of it, and to let me have it back, for you may imagine how much I value it.

You will observe that this took place at the end of the

year 1812, and early in 1813 he requested to see me, and told me of the situation of assistant in the laboratory of the Royal Institution, then just vacant.

At the same time that he thus gratified my desires as to scientific employment, he still advised me not to give up the prospects I had before me, telling me that Science was a harsh mistress, and in a pecuniary point of view, but poorly rewarding those who devoted themselves to her service. He smiled at my notion of the superior moral feelings of philosophic men, and said he would leave me to the experience of a few years to set me right on that matter. . . .

As a matter of fact, Faraday heard four of Davy's lectures, making careful notes which he wrote out in great detail. He included drawings which he made of the apparatus used by Davy in the demonstrations. Then he bound all of these pages together in a quarto volume—the same "quarto" that Faraday speaks of in his letter above. This very famous book is still on display at the Royal Institution.

At the time, Faraday was quite depressed about his bleak future in bookbinding and, with the expiration of his apprenticeship, saw no hope of getting into the field of science.

Davy received these notes at the very period when he was suffering from the effects of the nitrogen trichloride experiments. Instead of throwing the notes away or ignoring them, he must have looked at them with some care, for he took time on the day before Christmas to write to Faraday:

Sir, I am far from displeased with the proof you have given me of your confidence, and which displays great zeal, power of memory, and attention. I am obliged to go out of town, and shall not be settled in town till the end of January; I will then see you at any time you wish.

It would gratify me to be of any service to you. I wish it may be in my power.

Faraday did get a chance to meet Davy, although at that time there was no position open which could be offered to Faraday. In fact, Davy advised Faraday to stick to bookbinding and agreed to send much of the Institution's business his way. There is also evidence that Faraday even spent a few days as Davy's secretary during Davy's difficulty with his eye.

Then an emergency arose in the Royal Institution. Davy's assistant at that time was a man called Payne. Payne had taken a dislike to Mr. Newman, the instrument maker at the Institution, and the two men argued incessantly. One day Payne lost his temper. He rushed over to the startled Newman and struck him. It was a blow which would make scientific history!

Payne was promptly dismissed, and this left a vacancy at the Royal Institution.

Shortly thereafter, Faraday's widowed mother was startled one night when the clatter of horses' hooves echoed outside the door of their humble house. Sir Humphry Davy's coach had pulled up and a footman was knocking at the door. Since Faraday was upstairs in bed, the footman left a note requesting the young man to call on Sir Humphrey the next morning. The startled Mrs. Faraday could only mumble in amazement.

The meeting was a successful one. The result of it was that Davy recommended that the position vacated by Mr. Payne be offered to Michael Faraday.

When the members passed the resolution to employ Faraday, in 1813, they could hardly know they were hiring the man who would discover electromagnetic induction and its specific inductive capacity. In the year 1831 Faraday was to produce electric force by moving a conductor in an electric field, thus opening the way for the development of the dynamo. He was also to contribute vastly to the fields of electrolysis and the liquefaction of many gases, including chlorine.

As Davy's assistant, Faraday soon discovered that his position was hardly without excitement. Davy was immersed in his work with fluorine, which was still resisting his attempts to isolate it, and with the explosive nitrogen trichloride.

On April 9, 1813, Faraday described a wild laboratory experience to his friend Abbott:

I have escaped (not quite unhurt) from four different and strong explosions of the substance. Of these the most terrible was when I was holding between my thumb and finger a small tube containing 7½ grains of it. My face was within twelve inches of the tube; but I fortunately had on a glass mask. The explosion was so rapid as to blow my hand open, tear off a part of one nail, and has made my fingers so sore that I cannot yet use them easily. The pieces of tube were projected with such force as to cut the glass face of the mask I had on. On repeating the experiment this morning, the tube and a receiver were blown to pieces. I got a cut on my eyelid, and Sir H. bruised his hand.

The experiment was repeated again with a larger portion of the substance. It stood for a moment or two, and then exploded with a fearful noise; both Sir H. and I had masks on, but I escaped this time the best. Sir H. had his face cut in two places about the chin, and a violent blow on the forehead struck with a considerable thickness of silk and leather; and with this experiment he has for the present concluded.

But a far greater explosive mixture was about to be rubbed together—people. Sir Humphry and his temperamental Lady Davy prepared to sail for the continent of Europe. By chance, Sir Humphry's valet backed out of the trip at the last moment. To Lady Davy's disgust and disappointment, she found herself not only making the trip with her husband's portable chemical chest, but she found that her husband's substitute valet was none other than the Royal Institution's laboratory assistant, Michael Faraday.

CHAPTER SEVENTEEN

Davy Conquers France

The trip to Europe planned by Sir Humphry and Lady Davy was scheduled for the autumn of 1813. Davy had recently resigned as chemistry professor at the Royal Institution and Mr. William Brande had been appointed his successor. This apparently did not leave Davy free to socialize in London, since he agreed to continue research and to report the results of his research to the Royal Institution.

Meanwhile, Lady Davy was finding out how difficult marriage could be to a man whose interests were often elsewhere. Frequently she would find herself at social events without him. No longer was she the gay, sought-after widow of the past season. In truth, fishing, hunting, and chemistry were far from her idea of living a happy life. Thus, the plan to make a grand tour of Europe brightened her interests and she looked forward with great eagerness to a social conquest of the Continental capitals.

Somehow Davy obtained permission from Napoleon Bonaparte to pass through France. Since France and England were then at war, to visit France was not only an unusual request to make, but a unique privilege to have been granted. The reason may have been that Napoleon, just back from his disastrous retreat from Moscow, may have had some hope that Davy's experimental work with explosives could be made militarily useful to France.

At any rate, Sir Humphry went ahead with his plans. He promptly requested permission from the managers of the Royal Institution for Michael Faraday to accompany him on his "scientific travels." Mr. Brande of the Institution agreed to permit Faraday to go.

The party that crossed the English Channel that October consisted of Sir Humphry and Lady Davy, Michael Faraday, and Lady Davy's maid. They arrived in France only to be promptly arrested!

It took a week to put the matter right. Various authorities had to be contacted and passports had to be checked. Finally all was cleared and on October 27, 1813, they arrived safely in Paris. The warm reception they received more than made up for the week's detainment.

Humphry Davy's most ardent wish was to meet André Ampère, who had been a strong supporter of Davy as history's greatest chemist. But Ampère was not in Paris at this time. In his absence many French scientists did rush to pay homage to the noted scientist of their enemy country. As for Lady Davy, it was a dull round of banquets and receptions, most of them given in her husband's honor and nearly all of them in the company of scientists.

On November 2 Sir Humphry was the guest at a meeting of the French Institute and was honored by sitting at the right hand of the President. On November 5 Ampère returned to Paris particularly to meet Davy.

On November 10 Davy dined with Count Rumford. It had been ten years since the two men had last met. Rumford, it will be remembered, was the man who would not permit Davy to lecture at the Royal Institution until he had proved himself. Now the tables were turned. Davy was at the very height of his scientific eminence. Rumford was a disappointed, disillusioned man only eight months from death, a death hurried "by his wife's spiteful persecutions."

On November 23 André Ampère brought to Davy a sample of a new substance with which Gay-Lussac was working. It was a material which the French scientist Courtois had obtained from seaweed two years before. For some time the French chemists had been trying to determine its secrets. Despite the distractions of Paris, Davy managed to accomplish this in three weeks!

The substance, of course, was iodine. On December 6 Gay-Lussac presented a note to the French Institute suggesting that it was either an element or a compound of oxygen and that it was very similar to chlorine.

On December 13, 1813, Davy was elected a Corresponding Member of the First Class of the French Institute. At this meeting he read a paper giving a general view of the character of iodine. His paper, entitled "Some Experiments and Observations on a New Substance Which Becomes a Violet-Colored Gas by Heat," was read on January 20, 1814, to the Royal Society in London. In this well-done report, he explained the physical and chemical properties of iodine and the preparation of many compounds of iodine.

Davy's thoroughness as a chemist is nowhere better demonstrated than in this paper. First Davy explained why he was working on the same material Gay-Lussac was studying, clearly not forgetting Gay-Lussac's work with the metals of the alkalies that he himself had discovered. He then drew attention to the peculiarities of the combination of the new substance with silver; this, he showed, is markedly different from silver chloride. He then went on to form this compound synthetically: he formed the combination with potassium by direct union, describing its properties; studied the action of chlorine on the new substance (noting the formation of the yellow solid chloride and the mode of its decomposition by water) ; prepared a number of metallic compounds; studied the action of the new substance on phosphorus, and the nature of the product, including its mode of decomposition by water, with formation of the white crystalline phosphonium iodide and hydriodic acid gas. By acting on this gas with potassium Davy showed that it yields half its volume of hydrogen and forms the same product as by the direct union of the alkali metal with the new substance.

Davy further found that this gas is formed when the new substance and hydrogen are passed through a heated tube; it has a very strong attraction for water, which dissolves it to a large extent, and the concentrated solution rapidly becomes tawny. When the new substance is treated with potash solution, it forms the same product as by its direct union with potassium, together with a salt precisely similar to potassium hyperoxymuriate, and which, like that salt, is decomposed when heated, giving off oxygen.

Davy then went on to show that the new substance is expelled from its compounds when these are heated with chlorine. In addition, he studied the nature of the black fulminating compound (discovered by Desormes and Clement) by its action on the new substance with solution of ammonia, concluding that it was analogous to the detonating oil of Dulong. Davy also attempted to determine the combining proportion of the new substance, on the assumption that its compounds are analogous to those of chlorine, but had to admit that his experiments were made upon quantities too small to afford exact results. Nevertheless, they proved that the value is much higher than those of the simple inflammable bodies, and higher even than those of most of the metals. Sir Humphry further showed that the combination with hydrogen must be one of the heaviest elastic fluids existing.

Thus, despite the small amount of material he had to work with, and in spite of personal interruptions, Humphry Davy, working in borrowed laboratory and hotel room, managed to solve with unerring precision the problem of iodine:

> From all the facts that have been stated, there is every reason to consider this new substance as an undecompounded body. In its specific gravity, luster, color, and the high number in which it enters into combination, it resembles the metals; but in all its chemical agencies it is more analogous to oxygen and chlorine; it is a nonconductor of electricity, and possesses, like these bodies, the negative electrical energy with respect to metals, inflammable and alkaline substances, and hence when combined with substances in aqueous solution and electrized in the voltaic circuit, it separates at the positive surface; but it has a positive energy with respect to chlorine. . . . It agrees with chlorine and fluorine in forming acids with hydrogen.

All this did not make Humphry Davy very popular with Gay-Lussac. Gay-Lussac, of course, was extremely angry that Ampère had given Davy the material to work with. Davy later explained that he himself had given Gay-Lussac the idea that iodine was an element.

In any case, Sir Humphry was not the most tactful man alive. He managed to give everyone the feeling that the French chemists were inferior to the English. Even the Emperor Napoleon heard this story. Actually, Napoleon and Davy never met, although the Davys were presented at court to the Empress Marie Louise.

On December 29, 1813, after a two-month stay, Davy, having plainly outworn his welcome in Paris, set off with his entourage for the south of France and the Mediterranean.

CHAPTER EIGHTEEN

The European Tour

During the Davys' European travels, the unhappy Lady Davy turned her anger on Michael Faraday. Unable to compete with her husband's interest in chemistry, she could and did attack the "substitute valet." Racking her brain to find the most menial tasks for him to do, she ordered him to perform them in a voice calculated to anger the young man.

Previously, Davy had promised Faraday that he should no longer have to act as valet when they reached Paris, for there they would be able to engage a suitable servant. But in Paris they did not find one, and Faraday later wrote to a friend:

> At Lyons he could not get one; at Montpelier he could not get one; nor at Genoa, nor at Florence, nor at Rome, nor in all Italy; and I believe at last he did not wish to get one; and we are just the same now as we were when we left England. This of course throws things into my

116

duty which it was not my agreement, and is not my wish, to perform, but which are, if I remain with Sir H., unavoidable. These, it is true, are very few; for having been accustomed in early years to do for himself, he continues to do so at present and he leaves very little for a valet to perform: and as he knows that it is not pleasing to me, and that I do not consider myself as obliged to do them, he is always as careful as possible to keep those things from me which he knows would be disagreeable. But Lady Davy is of another humor. She likes to show her authority, and at first I found her extremely earnest in mortifying me. This occasioned quarrels between us, at each of which I gained ground, and she lost it; for the frequency made me care nothing about them, and weakened her authority, and after each she behaved in a milder manner.

The bad blood between Lady Davy and Faraday extended far beyond a mere exchange of words. They actually hated each other. Faraday had been brought up in a very strict religious sect and he viewed Lady Davy as a social parasite. As for Lady Davy, she never regarded Faraday with anything but contempt—a poor low-class guttersnipe who represented the sphere of activities which distracted her husband.

In another letter Faraday complained:

> I should have but little to complain of were I traveling with Sir Humphry alone, or were Lady Davy like him; but her temper makes it oftentimes go wrong with me, with herself, and with Sir H.

The truth is that Sir Humphry had begun to perceive that Faraday was something more than a mere bottle washer or menial servant. Certainly Davy was to notice before this Continental voyage was over that young Faraday—far from being a tinkerer and mechanic—was actually a scientist in his own right. And realizing this, it may have been that Davy was slowly developing the jealousy that was to mark his later attitude toward Faraday.

At any rate, desperate now, Faraday wrote to a friend back in England that he was thinking of returning home, even to going back to bookbinding. But Faraday stuck it out.

While they were in Geneva, Sir Humphry and his party were guests of the distinguished Swiss Professor de La Rive. They used to go shooting since La Rive and Davy were both sportsmen. Michael Faraday would always come along and load Davy's gun. He also took his meals with the servants. When La Rive found out that the modest Faraday was actually Davy's laboratory assistant and not his servant, he was quite disturbed and proposed that Faraday dine with the family. Lady Davy, however, refused to permit this and La Rive resolved the dilemma by sending Faraday's meals to his rooms.

Humphry Davy continued his experiments on iodine as they traveled and, in Geneva, he made a series of studies on the "torpedo fish" or electric eel. In Florence,

Davy worked on the combustion of diamond which he discovered formed a gas indistinguishable from the gas evolved from burning charcoal—hence Davy concluded that diamond must be pure carbon. In addition, he made use of the great burning glass which had been used for many years after being introduced by Cosmo III, Grand Duke of Tuscany. The story goes that the peppery Humphry Davy bounced around so quickly they feared their great burning glass would not survive; but it did.

In May the party went to Naples, and Davy began a series of ascents of Mount Vesuvius. When the time came to leave, he asked the guide to write him regularly concerning the changing conditions of the volcano and, although the guide insisted on addressing his letters to Davy, "Siromfredevi—Londra," the reports did reach him at the Royal Institution.

Davy traveled back to Rome and then went on to northern Italy. At Milan he met the great Alessandro Volta who was then almost seventy years old. This was the man for whom the voltaic pile was named, the source of electrical power that had made so many of Davy's discoveries possible.

Three months were then spent at Geneva. Lady Davy may then have had her greatest pleasure, for many of the people she had met in earlier times were there. As for the war, Paris had fallen and Napoleon was now a prisoner on the island of Elba. Humphry Davy continued to experiment on iodine and spent his leisure time fishing. While he did take part in some of the social life, Lady Davy must have done a great deal of visiting without him. The beautiful countryside of Italy had stimulated Davy to write a good deal of poetry at this time.

Davy left Switzerland to spend the winter in Italy and his trip took him through Bavaria and the Tirol. On October 6, 1814, he was at Innsbruck and his impressions of the grand scenery are described in his notebook. On his way to Rome he crossed the Apennines.

One day at Pietramala, in the middle of the towering mountains many thousands of feet above sea level, Davy happened to see a column of flame shooting toward the sky. It seemed to burn perpetually. Davy had some of the air that he had observed coming out of the openings collected. When this air was ignited, it burned with the same kind of flame as the great column he had first seen. He collected more of it in order to subject it to chemical analysis.

When Sir Humphry reached Florence, he studied the gas closely and found it to be "carburated hydrogen," similar to coal gas. Davy's conclusion was that there must be a bed of coal acted on by underground heat which caused the gas to appear. At this very time, the miners in England were trying to find someone who would help them solve the problem of their mine explosions, and it was to be Davy's work on this same coal gas that was later to aid in the solution.

Davy reached Rome on November 2, 1814, and stayed in the Italian capital until March 1, 1815. In addition to his chemical experiments, he also had a great opportunity to shoot wildfowl. He continued to forward to the Royal Society the results of his experiments, and these were published in the "Philosophical Transactions" for 1815 under the following titles:

"Some Experiments and Observations on the Colors Used in Paintings by the Ancients"—January 14;

"Some Experiments on a Solid Compound of Iodine and Oxygen, and on its Chemical Agencies"—February 10;

"On the Action of Acids on the Salts Usually Called the Hyperoxymuriates, and on the Gases Produced from Them"—February 15.

The first of these papers examined the composition of ancient colors. In it, Sir Humphry founded the chemical basis of the reds, yellows, and blues.

Vesuvius was erupting and Davy hastened to make several more ascents for scientific purposes. Again he communicated the results of his investigations on volcanic eruption to the Royal Society.

About this time the Davys' projected plan for traveling to the Near East and Turkey was suddenly canceled. Plague had broken out in Malta and in the Levant. Then word came that Napoleon had escaped from Elba. A new period of war threatened to engulf Europe.

The Davys hurried home, bypassing France by going through Germany and Belgium. They arrived in England on April 23, 1815, after having been gone for nearly eighteen months.

Davy wrote his mother on his arrival:

> We have had a very agreeable and instructive journey and Lady Davy agrees with me in thinking that England is the only country to *live* in, however interesting it may be to *see* other countries.
>
> I yesterday bought a good house in Grosvenor Street, and we shall sit down in this happy land.

Faraday, too, was glad—and relieved—to get back to England. He was again engaged as superintendent of the apparatus and assistant in the laboratory of the Royal Institution, at a salary of thirty shillings a week.

Then in June of 1815, just a few weeks after Davy's return to England, Newbottle Colliery exploded with fifty-seven men and boys killed in the coal mines. A short time later a similar disaster occurred at Sheriff Hill.

CHAPTER NINETEEN

The Development of the Safety Lamp

In the English coal mining regions, the number of mine explosions was increasing and far more deaths were occurring.

The reason for this was that the iron trade had grown enormously and, with it, there developed a great need for more coal to supply power. In addition, new tools were being produced to work the mines. Improvements in the steam engine had made it possible to pump out flooded mines and to bring up more coal. Consequently, it was now possible to mine deeper into the bowels of the earth.

No longer were the pits shallow as in the early days of coal mining and, as the mine shafts were sunk deeper, occasional explosions due to firedamp gas resulted. As the pits deepened and side tunnels were dug, explosions became more frequent. Sometimes the combustible gas called firedamp became so thick that the men could not work in certain areas. The miners then carried candles, thus creating the danger of igniting an explosive mixture of mine gases.

In the previous century it had been believed that the inflammable gases were sulfurous and, in the year 1732, attempts had been made to air out the coal pits by using furnaces and mechanical sweepers. Also, the invention of a sparking wheel—flint on a rotating steel disk which threw a shower of sparks so that the miners could work by the light—did not stop the mounting casualty lists.

John Buddle, a contemporary authority on coal mine ventilation, wrote:

> . . . the hopes of this society ever seeing its most desirable object accomplished must rest upon the event of some method being discovered of producing such a chemical change upon carbureted hydrogen gas as to render it innoxious as fast as it is discharged, or as it approaches the neighborhood of lights. In this view of the subject, it is to scientific men only that we must look up for assistance in providing a cheap and effectual remedy.

In seeking such a remedy, the Royal Society had received many suggestions. Some of these, however, turned out to be of the crackpot variety. One of them, for example, recommended by a Dr. Trotter, proposed to ~~od~~ the mines with chlorine gas—which would have ~~oned~~ the miners!

~~was~~ a clergyman, the Reverend Dr. Gray, later the

Bishop of Bristol and a member of the Society seeking remedies for the mining disasters, who learned that Sir Humphry Davy had returned to England. Dr. Gray wrote to Davy to implore him to help the miners.

Davy was in Melrose enjoying the shooting when he received Gray's message. Sir Humphry was delighted to respond, and his reply to Gray was:

> It will give me great satisfaction if my chemical knowledge can be of any use in an inquiry so interesting to humanity, and I beg you will assure the committee of my readiness to cooperate with them in any experiments or investigations on the subject.
>
> If you think by visiting the mines can be of any use, I will cheerfully do so.
>
> I shall be here ten days longer, and on my return south, will visit any place you will be kind enough to point out to me, where I may be able to acquire information on the subject of coal gas.

Accordingly, Davy visited with Mr. John Buddle who was overjoyed at Sir Humphry's willingness to undertake the study. Buddle wrote to Dr. Gray on August 24, 1815:

> Permit me to offer my best acknowledgments for the opportunity which your attention to the cause of humanity has afforded me of being introduced to Sir Humphry Davy.

By early October Davy had already experimented with several of the airtight lamps that had been suggested at various times and had analyzed quantities of firedamp which had been furnished him.

On October 15 Davy wrote to a Mr. Hodgson:

> My experiments are going on successfully and I hope in a few days to send you an account of them; I am going to be fortunate far beyond my expectations.

In trying to find a way of illuminating the mines, Davy rejected the idea of an airtight container for a candle. Nor had he been able to find a way of generating a gas that would neutralize the firedamp in a mine. However, he did find that he could make a lantern with solid sides, with apertures on the bottom so that the flames would not get to the atmosphere. He had also observed what any boy who has ever handled wire gauze in a flame now knows—that the flame cannot pass through the small openings of the screen.

On October 19 Davy wrote to Hodgson:

> . . . explosive mixtures of minedamp will not pass through small apertures or tubes; and . . . if a lamp or lantern be made airtight on the sides, and furnished with apertures to admit the air, it will not communicate flame the outward atmosphere.

October 30, 1815, he wrote Dr. Gray:

The Development of the Safety Lamp

As it was the consequence of your invitation that I endeavored to investigate the nature of the firedamp, I owe to you the first notice of the progress of my experiments.

My results have been successful far beyond my expectations. I shall enclose a little sketch of my views on the subject; and I hope in a few days to be able to send a paper with the apparatus for the committee. I trust the safe lamp will answer all the objects of the colliery.

I consider this at present as a private communication. I wish you to examine the lamps I have had constructed, before you give any account of my labors to the committee.

I have never received so much pleasure from the result of any of my chemical labors; for I trust the cause of humanity will gain something by it.

However, it seems that the letter—against Davy's wishes—was shown around, for an extract of it appeared in Dunn's *View of the Coal Trade*.

On November 9 Humphry Davy read his first paper on the subject to the Royal Society, entitled "On the Firedamp of Coal Mines, and on the Methods of Lighting the Mines so as to Prevent Its Explosion." In it, he told of how his attention had been called to the subject and how his experiments with different forms of phosphorus and with electric light in closed lanterns were to no avail. Davy also discussed the explosive nature and combustibility of firedamp, but pointed out that it differed from most inflammable gases in that it required a very high temperature before it could be ignited. In addition, he found out that the flame formed by a certain mixture of air and firedamp failed to pass through tubes of narrow diameter. And, in comparing tubes of metal and of glass, he observed that the flame passed through glass tubes of smaller diameter. Explosions were stopped by metallic tubes of one-fifth of an inch when they were one and a half inches long. Davy also stated that wire gauze could stop the explosion.

Sir Humphry apparently did not know that other scientists, notably Wollaston and Tennant, had already observed that mixtures of air and coal gas would not explode in very narrow tubes.

In his paper of November 9 Davy suggested that:

> . . . It is evident then, that to prevent explosions in coal mines, it is only necessary to use airtight lanterns, supplied with air from tubes or canals of small diameter, or from apertures covered with wire gauze placed below the flame, through which explosions cannot be communicated, and having a chimney at the upper part, as a similar system for carrying off the foul air; and common lanterns may be easily adapted to the purpose by being made airtight in the door and sides, by being furnished with the chimney and the system of safety apertures below and above. The principle being known, it is easy to adapt and multiply practical applications of it.

He then went on to devise several lamps on this principle, trying them out with very explosive mixtures.

Davy's second paper on the subject was read on January 11, 1816. It was called "An Account of an Invention for Giving Light in Explosive Mixtures of Firedamp in Coal Mines by Consuming the Firedamp." In this paper he showed how the tubes as well as the sides of the lantern could be replaced by wire gauze. The firedamp enters through the wire gauze from outside with ease, burning with a bright flame, but no explosion passes outward.

In Sir Humphry's third paper to the Royal Institution, "On the Combustion of Explosive Mixtures Confined by Wire Gauze, with Some Observations on Flame," he explained his work concerning the limits of size of apertures in the wire gauze and discussed the lowering of the temperature of the explosive mixture below the ignition point. Further, he pointed out that lamps in which flames are enclosed in a cylinder of gauze had already been tried in two of the most dangerous mines near Newcastle with perfect success.

Several people had already tried the safety lamp, or "Davy lamp" as it was called, and their enthusiasm was high. John Buddle, who took one of the Davy lamps into Wall's End Colliery, wrote:

> I first tried it in an explosive mixture on the surface; and then took it into a mine; it is impossible for me to express my feelings at the time when I first suspended the lamp in the mine and saw it red hot. I said to those around me "We have at last subdued this monster."

Later, Humphry Davy, anxious to see for himself how the lamp worked, went down into the West End Colliery on June 1, 1816. He was delighted with the results.

From one of the grateful coal mine directors, Davy received this appreciative letter:

After having introduced your safety lamp into general use in all the collieries under my direction where inflammable air prevails, and after using them daily in every variety of explosive mixture, for upwards of three months, I feel the highest possible gratification in stating to you that they have answered to my entire satisfaction.

The safety of the lamps is so easily proved by taking them into any part of a mine charged with firedamp, and all the explosive gradations of that dangerous element are so easily and satisfactorily ascertained by their application, as to strike the minds of the most prejudiced with the strongest conviction of their high utility; and our colliers have adopted them with the greatest eagerness.

Besides the facilities afforded by this invention to the working of coal mines abounding in firedamp, it has enabled the directors and superintendents to ascertain, with the utmost precision and expedition, both the presence, the quantity, and the correct situation of the gas. Instead of creeping inch by inch with a candle, as is usual, along the galleries of a mine suspected to contain firedamp in order to ascertain its presence, we walk firmly in with the safe lamps, and with the utmost confidence prove the actual state of the mine. By observing attentively the several appearances upon the flame of the lamp, in an examination of this kind, the cause of accidents which have happened to the most experienced and cautious miners is completely developed; and this has been, in a great measure, matter of mere conjecture.

I feel peculiar satisfaction in dwelling upon a subject which is of the utmost importance, not only to the great cause of humanity, and to the mining interest of the country, but also to the commercial and manufacturing interests of the United Kingdom; for I am convinced that by the happy invention of the safe lamp large proportions of the coal mines of the empire will be rendered available, which otherwise might have remained inaccessible, at least without an invention of similar utility, which could not have been wrought without much loss of the mineral, and risk of life and capital.

It is not necessary that I should enlarge upon the national advantages which must necessarily result from an invention calculated to prolong our supply of mineral coal, because I think them obvious to every reflecting mind; but I cannot conclude, without expressing my highest sentiments of admiration for those talents which have developed the properties, and controlled the power, of one of the most dangerous elements which human enterprise has hitherto had to encounter.

If Davy was moved by this letter, he received another from the miners at Whitehaven Collieries which moved him even more:

We, the undersigned, miners at the Whitehaven Collieries, belonging to the Earl of Lonsdale, return our sincere thanks to Sir Humphry Davy, for his invaluable discovery of the safe lamps, which are to us life preservers;

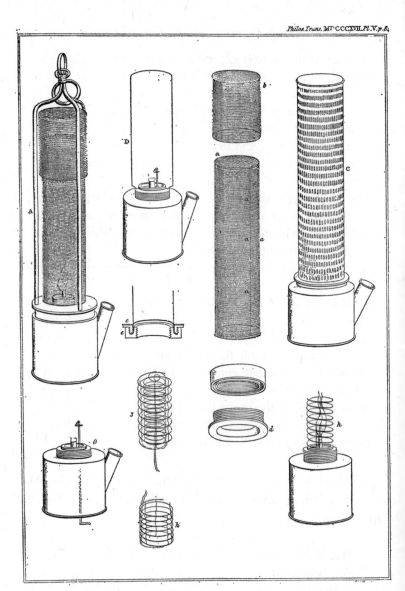

Components of the miner's safety lamp, from the Transactions
of the Royal Society, 1817. (Courtesy of The Burndy Library)

and being the only return in our power to make, we most humbly offer this, our tribute of gratitude.

This letter contained the names of eighty-two miners; forty-seven of them, unable to write, had made a cross next to their names.

While many of his friends urged him to do so, Humphry Davy never sought to protect his invention of the safety lamp with a patent. John Buddle felt that he could have received $25,000 to $50,000 a year from this patent alone.

But Davy chose not to:

> My Good Friend,
> I never thought of such a thing: my sole object was to serve the cause of humanity; and if I have succeeded, I am amply rewarded in the gratifying reflection of having done so. . . . More wealth could not increase either my fame or my happiness. It might undoubtedly enable me to put four horses to my carriage; but what would it avail me to have it said that Sir Humphry drives his carriage and four!

Curiously enough, a great wrangle now began over who actually did have the prior invention. Many people believed that the basic invention had been George Stephenson's.* Humphry Davy, who felt very magnanimous about his gesture of "giving the safety lamp to

* George Stephenson, the son of a fireman, was born near Newcastle in 1781. He had a hard struggle to educate himself and work up to the position of engineer at Killingworth Pit. It was several years after the great safety lamp controversy that Stephenson developed his first locomotive. He died in 1848.

humanity," was incensed over the claims of the upstart Stephenson.

Plans to hold a public meeting of gratitude to Davy, with the presentation of a plate service, were postponed while authorities tried to determine the priority of claims.

Humphry Davy's anger over this situation finally reached the boiling point. One of his milder reactions went like this:

> I never heard a word of George Stephenson and his lamps till six weeks after my principle of security had been published; and the general impression of the scientific men in London, which is confirmed by what I heard at Newcastle, is that Stephenson had some loose idea floating in his mind, which he had unsuccessfully attempted to put in practice till after my labors were made known; then, he made something like a safe lamp, except that it is not safe, for the apertures below are four times, and those above twenty times too large; but, even if Stephenson's plans had not been posterior to my principles, still there is no analogy between his glass exploding machine, and my metallic tissue permeable to light and air, and impermeable to flame.

Davy's friends were even angrier than he was, largely due to the fact that Stephenson was relatively unknown while Davy was recognized as the leading scientist of his day. They could hardly have known that the locomotive was taking shape in the head of the man they refused to believe was an inventor.

One of Davy's biographers, T. E. Thorpe, a great admirer of Stephenson, believed that Stephenson most certainly was working on a means of protecting a flame in coal mines. But he was also certain that the crude ideas with which he worked did not compare with Davy's intuitive leap to the basic principle of the safety lamp.

On September 25, 1817, Davy returned from Scotland and went to Newcastle where a dinner service of gold plate worth $12,000 was presented to him by the grateful mine operators. Humphry Davy specified in his will that the gold service should be melted down after his death, and made into a medal for the Royal Society to reward "the most important discovery annually in chemistry in Europe or Anglo-America."

Davy was further stimulated in working with the safety lamp to study the peculiarities of flame, its luminosity, and burning mixture, and eventually he succeeded in constructing a flameless lamp.

Early in the summer of 1818, Davy again went abroad. On this trip he wrote his mother:

> We are just going on a very interesting journey. I am first to visit the coal miners of Flanders, who have sent me a very kind letter of invitation and of thanks for saving their lives. We are then going to Austria, where I shall show Vienna to Lady Davy, and visit the mines; and lastly, before I return, we are going to visit Naples.
>
> I have the commands of His Royal Highness the Prince Regent to make experiments upon some very interesting

Davy explaining the principle of the safety lamp. (The Bettmann Archive)

ancient manuscripts, which I hope to unfold. I had yesterday the honor of an audience from His Royal Highness, and he commissioned me to pursue this object in the most gracious and kind manner. . . .

Meanwhile, a curious situation developed that added more trouble to the hassle over Stephenson's prior claims for the safety lamp. Deaths in the coal mines did not go down.

What actually happened was that the safety lamp made it possible for the coal tunnels to be dug deeper, so that more dangerous mines were worked. Also, miners felt secure with the safety lamp and may have become careless. In addition, when the wire gauze of the safety lamps became red hot, it was very possible that the flame was able to leap through and thus cause an explosion.

Soon a parliamentary committee was called to inquire about the safety lamp. Was it possible that the device would be dangerous under certain conditions? Michael Faraday, called on to testify about this, replied in his honest, straightforward way that they could indeed be dangerous. Although he was completely loyal to Humphry Davy, he had to tell the truth. Davy was outraged and angry but Faraday stuck to his guns. Sir Humphry was never able to forgive Faraday for making this testimony.

CHAPTER TWENTY

President of the Royal Society

In October of 1818 Sir Humphry Davy was made a baronet. While other honors were to come his way, the years of his great scientific contributions were over.

In Naples, on a later trip to the Continent, Sir Humphry began his researches on the Herculaneum manuscripts. These manuscripts were badly stuck together and it was nearly impossible to unfold them. Most people believed that the manuscripts had suffered due to fire, but Davy became convinced that the passage of time had transformed the vegetable matter of the paper into the dark, coal-like manuscripts.

The method Davy used to try to unroll these precious documents was a clever one. Convinced that the solid mass of manuscripts was due to a chemical change during a fermentation process of the vegetable matter, he was tempted to try chlorine on the cemented pages. Since chlorine could combine with hydrogen, it might be possible to destroy the adhesive matter without affecting the papyrus of which the scroll was made. He tried this and obtained an immediate reaction, although the museum curators looked on in horror while the papyrus smoked. As soon as Davy applied heat, the layers began to peel away from each other, and the letters appeared much more distinct.

Although he managed to unroll a number of the manuscripts and communicated his results to the Royal Society, the curators of the museum did not appear to appreciate his efforts. Davy, of course, was very resentful.

Traveling with Lady Davy, his portable chemistry chest, and his fishing equipment, Sir Humphry left Naples to try the hot baths at Lucca. It was not long before he analyzed the mineral content of the water there. The results of his analysis were published in the *Memoirs* of the Royal Academy of Science of Naples, whereupon he was elected a member of that organization.

Later, the Davys traveled north, but with the approach of winter they returned to Naples. Sir Humphry's brother John was now an army surgeon in Ceylon and Humphry Davy wrote his mother on March 13, 1820, expressing the hope that both he and John could be with her in Penzance at the end of May.

The visit never came about, and Lady Davy never did meet her husband's mother and sisters. As it happened, Davy arrived in London much later—in June.

On the nineteenth of that month, Sir Joseph Banks died. This distinguished gentleman had been President of the Royal Society for forty-two years. Sir Joseph was born in London in 1743, had gone to Harrow, Eton, and Oxford, and had inherited in 1761, at the age of eighteen, a vast fortune from his father. He became an explorer and naturalist, traveling to Labrador and Newfoundland in 1766. He was with James Cook in the famous around-the-world voyage of 1768–71, and he was in Iceland in 1772.

In 1778, before Humphry Davy was born, Banks became President of the Royal Society. The important herbarium which Sir Joseph Banks developed had a worldwide significance and it is now a part of the British Museum. Banks also had a magnificent library on natural history, which has also become a part of the museum.

As a man known to scientists all over the world, Banks had become a very strong force in the exchange of scientific ideas. A knight commander of the Bath, and a member of the privy council, he raised the status of science considerably in Great Britain.

It was shortly after Sir Joseph's death had been announced that Humphry Davy boldly declared that he was a candidate for the vacant chair of President of the Royal Society. Davy himself had been elected to the Royal Society in 1803 when he was twenty-five years old, and had in 1805 received its coveted Copley medal. He had also been Secretary until his marriage in 1812.

Four years later, in 1816, he had received the Rumford medal for his work on the safety lamp.

Sir Joseph Banks apparently had wished the office of President to go to Dr. William Hyde Wollaston.* This preference was also that of many of the members of the Royal Society. It is possible that Humphry Davy's public announcement to campaign for office was regarded by the older members as not in the best taste. Indeed, Sir Joseph himself had already indicated that Davy was "rather too lively to fill the chair of the Royal Society with that degree of gravity" which it should have.

As matters turned out, however, Wollaston declined the nomination and Davy was elected by a "strong majority," over a "more aristocratic candidate, Lord Colchester."

For the next seven years, in fact until his failing health obliged him to resign, Sir Humphry Davy was reelected to the office of President of the Royal Society without opposition.

The President's chair turned out to be a difficult job for Davy. His quick temper, lack of tact, and tendency to act on sudden impulse were the very opposite of the traits which Sir Joseph Banks had displayed as President.

Moreover, an institution known as the "weekly conversation," which the Fellows had enjoyed at the

* William Hyde Wollaston (1766–1828) was an English chemist who proved the identity of frictional and voltaic electricity. He discovered a means of working platinum around 1804, and made a vast fortune from this process.

Bankses' home, did not have much success at Davy's house. Doubtless, Lady Davy was not sympathetic to it, and Davy himself found it difficult to organize the meetings effectively. Accordingly, they were transferred to the rooms of the Society. Gradually fewer and fewer members attended the "conversations" and eventually they were discontinued.

Perhaps Davy's greatest contributions as President of the Royal Society were the addresses that he delivered before that body. He was an eloquent lecturer and his speeches were memorable ones. Practically, however, the duties of the office began to limit his scientific time more and more, although he did try to spend some time in the laboratory.

In 1821 Sir Humphry published a paper in the *Philosophical Transactions* entitled, "On the Magnetic Phenomena Produced by Electricity," following it with a paper concerning electrical phenomena in a vacuum. In 1823 he wrote another paper on electromagnetism. These papers strongly suggest that Davy foresaw the great possibilities of electromagnetism. But he himself did not have the time to do the lengthy research in this field and it fell to Michael Faraday to make the great discoveries.

Unfortunately, in the years ahead, there were to be several serious clashes between Davy and Faraday, and Davy's part in them remains difficult to understand or to forgive.

CHAPTER TWENTY-ONE

Rivalry with Faraday

In 1821 Dr. William Wollaston had become excited over the discovery which Hans Christian Oersted * had made in Denmark the year before. This was the famous demonstration in which the magnetic needle of a compass is deflected when brought close to a current-carrying wire.

Humphry Davy was quite aware of Wollaston's work and he referred to Wollaston's observations in one of his papers on electromagnetism. In April, 1821, Wollaston tried out some of his ideas in Davy's laboratory. The experiments were unsuccessful, and while Davy and Wollaston were discussing them, Michael Faraday came in.

During the summer of 1821 Faraday began experi-

---

* Hans Christian Oersted, the discoverer of electromagnetism, lived from 1770 to 1851. He worked on the compressibility of liquids and gases, and in 1825 prepared metallic aluminum. It was during an evening lecture in April, 1820, that he noticed the moving of a magnetic needle in an electric field.

mental work on his own in this area and, by September, the young man had made his first great breakthrough in electromagnetism when he observed that a current-carrying wire suspended over a magnet would actually gyrate around it. This was something akin to the idea Wollaston had been trying out and which had not worked. The research was published in the October issue of the *Quarterly Journal of Science*.

The upshot of all this was that rumors began circulating that Faraday had stolen Wollaston's ideas, and it appeared that Sir Humphry Davy himself was spreading those rumors. Davy never denied this accusation outright, but Faraday invited Wollaston to witness his demonstration and the rumors then ceased.

The biographer T. E. Thorpe regrets Davy's greed for fame. He declares that "The jealousy thus manifested by Davy is one of the pitiful facts of his history." While Thorpe felt that this did not detract from Davy's genius as a scientist, it nevertheless lessened his stature as a person.

From our point of view today, it suggests that the great drive which Davy showed in his actions was actually a deep-seated hunger for success and recognition, although he distinctly possessed a delight in discovery for its own sake. It must be admitted, however, that this driving hunger rendered him less appreciative of the efforts of others, particularly in the areas in which he himself had pioneered. As we have seen, his reaction to the work of

Gay-Lussac and his general attitude toward the French chemists of the period are a reflection of this.

Later, Davy had another difficulty with Faraday. On March 5, 1823, Dr. Paris, whose contemporary biography of Davy is a critical one, visited Sir Humphry for dinner. Being somewhat early, he stopped at the Royal Institution laboratory, where he found Michael Faraday doing experiments with chlorine and chloral hydrate in closed tubes. Paris noted the oily matter in some of the tubes and chided Faraday about using dirty test tubes. Faraday looked at one of the tubes with great surprise, agreeing that it was indeed dirty. He picked it up and began to file off the sealed end.

Both men jumped as the material in the tube exploded.

When they studied the now open tube, the oily matter had vanished. Faraday was quite bewildered. He promptly repeated the experiment.

Paris, however, was obliged to hurry to Sir Humphry Davy's dinner. After dinner, he mentioned to Davy what he had observed in the laboratory. Davy knitted his brow and grew silent and thoughtful. Finally he told Paris that he would look into the experiment the next day.

The following morning Dr. Paris received a short note from Faraday, stating that the oily substance they had seen had turned out to be liquid chlorine.

Humphry Davy had had considerable experience with chlorine, as we already know. Exposing chlorine to a low temperature results in a solid substance, and, before 1810, it was generally believed that the solid substance was chlorine itself. Davy had showed the solid to be chloral hydrate. As a pure gas, chlorine could not be condensed at 40 degrees below zero Fahrenheit.

What Faraday had actually found, by heating crystals of chloral hydrate in a closed tube, was that he could obtain the liquid form of chlorine.

Davy's quick mind saw at once what this might mean and he rushed over to witness Faraday's condensation of chlorine. Davy then promptly called for a strong glass tube. He added ammonium chloride and sulfuric acid, sealed the tube, and watched the reaction. Hydrochloric acid evolved and condensed into a liquid. He repeated the experiment with carbonic acid gas and with nitrous oxide, as well as several other gases, and each experiment worked successfully.

When Faraday wrote up his experiment of the liquefaction of chlorine to the Royal Society a week later, Davy revised it. The result was that the report sounded as if Davy had predicted all the results and essentially claimed the experiment as his own. True, it was common practice at that time for senior professors to take credit for all the ideas and results of their juniors, but Faraday was not really a junior or a mere assistant. However, the mild-mannered Faraday was always very courteous to Davy concerning the matter, although it must have rankled somewhat.

The most painful incident between the two men

occurred when Faraday was proposed for membership in the Royal Society, for here Davy actively opposed him. Wollaston was one of Faraday's sponsors; indeed Faraday's was the first name on the list of proposals. Davy threw his full weight against him and, although we will never know who voted, there was one—and only one—blackball against Faraday, when the actual vote was taken.

Faraday himself told how vigorous was Davy's opposition:

> Sir H. Davy told me I must take down my certificate. I replied that I had not put it up; that I could not take it down, as it was put up by my proposers. He then said I must get my proposers to take it down. I answered that I knew they would not do so. Then he said, "I as President will take it down." I replied that I was sure Sir H. Davy would do what he thought was for the good of the Royal Society.

But Faraday would not allow himself to be intimidated and he was duly made a member of the Royal Society in January of 1824.

As for the aging Sir Humphry, he was not only in poor health, but other work was piling up on him. For one thing, he was in the midst of a new series of studies concerning metals. Also, the Admiralty had sought his advice in the fall of 1823 regarding the prevention of corrosion on the copper sheathing of ships.

In January of 1824, the same month Faraday was

made a member of the Royal Society, Davy wrote to his brother John:

> I have lately made a discovery of which you will for many reasons be glad. I have found a complete method of preserving the copper sheeting of ships, which now readily corrodes. It is by rendering it negatively electrical. My results are of the most beautiful and unequivocal kind; a mass of tin renders a surface of copper 200 or 300 times its own size sufficiently electrical to have no action on sea water.
>
> I was led to this discovery by principle, as you will easily imagine; and the saving to government and the country by it will be immense. I am going to apply it immediately to the navy. I might have made an immense fortune by a patent for this discovery, but I have given it to my country; for in everything connected with interest, I am resolved to live and die at least "sans tache."

Davy's great joy in this discovery was short-lived however. As soon as he had suggested that copper keels could be protected with bars of tin or zinc, people began to publicly doubt whether this could work. In fact, the idea was ridiculed. Nevertheless it was tried out. As it turned out, the copper was protected from corrosion. But, unfortunately, the uncorroded metal became such a bed of weeds and barnacles that the ship could not maintain speed.

Reacting to this, the public press now rose to heights of ridicule and sarcasm and Davy was belittled again and again. Because he was increasingly ill, Davy found it hard to recover from these blows—and there were more to come.

In September, 1826, Davy's mother died. Of her, the inscription in Ludgvan Church says that "She had lived long to rejoice with a meek and thankful spirit in the distinctions which rewarded the merits of her oldest child."

In 1826 Davy gave his last address before the Royal Society. His brother reports that Davy gasped as he spoke, beads of perspiration falling from his face. Those near him thought the famous man of science would collapse. He was unable to attend the dinner afterward. Yet it was at this meeting that he was elected President of the Royal Society for the seventh—and last—time.

CHAPTER TWENTY-TWO

The Last Days

In January, 1827, Sir Humphry Davy set out with his brother John for the warmer climate and rest which he might obtain in southern Europe. John Davy, who had been absent from England for four years until just the month before, had returned to find his brother partially paralyzed in his right side.

The Davy brothers bypassed bustling Paris and worked their way across the cold and frozen French countryside. One afternoon the wheels of their carriage became stuck in deep ruts. Stumbling down a hill on foot, Humphry Davy fell many times before they found a cottage where they were able to spend the night.

Winter remained with them through the Alps. The snows of northern Italy were very deep, delaying them longer, and it was not until the first week of March that they arrived at Ravenna. Here John Davy had to leave Humphry and return to Corfu to take up his duties as a physician in the army.

Davy spent the summer traveling alone in Italy. He

recovered somewhat, although a letter to Lady Davy fairly begged her to come to Europe to meet him.

Sir Humphry returned to London in October, 1827, and announced his resignation as President of the Royal Society. He was succeeded by his old friend and patron, Davies Gilbert.

Davy's book on fishing, *Salmonia, or Days of Fly Fishing,* was published in 1828. He had always loved this sport and had been an ardent admirer of the famous angler, Izaak Walton. Although many editions of *Salmonia* were published, it fell artistically short of Walton's *The Compleat Angler.*

In the spring of 1828 Davy returned to Europe. Here he wrote *Consolations in Travel, or the Last Days of a Philosopher.* He suffered a stroke while writing the second draft and was obliged to send for his brother who was then stationed at Malta with the army. The message was not delivered and Davy sent a second letter on February 23, 1829. He rallied after John Davy arrived, and Lady Davy finally joined them from England in early April. They traveled slowly to Geneva, arriving on May 28.

It was a beautiful spring day, with the green plant life surging out of the earth. Davy would spend hours contemplating the mountain landscape, taking great drafts of the warm, fresh air. Lake Geneva gleamed below him, promising to be a fisherman's paradise.

That evening the fifty-year-old Humphry Davy went to bed early, and never awakened.

CHAPTER TWENTY-THREE

Assessment of Davy's Contributions

Science made great strides in the fifty years that spanned Sir Humphry Davy's lifetime. Yet the contributions of a single individual are often lost as time passes. What, in reappraisal, were the accomplishments of this great man of English chemistry?

Davy's great fame as a stirring lecturer on chemical subjects is an established fact. His influence on both his colleagues and laymen in raising the dignity of science was beyond measure. His own discoveries in chemistry are part of the record. He found sodium and potassium, established the science of electrochemistry, and reported fundamental studies in nitrous oxide and chlorine. His work on the miners' safety lamp not only demonstrated that science has practical applications, but called to the world's attention the fact that scientists and their ideas can benefit mankind.

In Davy's later years the great drive for fame that

had sustained him for decades grew fainter. He could look back on the long busy road he had traveled so vigorously and feel comfort in moments of retrospect.

The little boy who dreamed on the rocks at Penzance, or marveled at the glorious Mounts Bay, could never have foreseen the fame and the accomplishment which lay ahead of him. The events which came about must have appeared like coincidences to him. He had leaped from a school where he spent little time studying, to a laboratory where study was crucial.

He remembered the kind Dr. Borlase, who had now become a surgeon and the disappointed Dr. Tonkin who wished that Davy had become a doctor. He recalled Davies Gilbert and Gregory Watt, whose stimulating conversations spurred his eagerness for knowledge.

Of course, the wonderful opportunity that brought Davy to Dr. Beddoes and the Pneumatic Institution, and which Davy capitalized upon, was an important part of his growth. Here he had met not only ideas in science, but the humanistic ideas of Coleridge, Southey, and Roget.

From the time of his father's death, Davy moved in four short years from an idle boy in a little town, with few thoughts and friends, to Chemical Superintendent of an urban experimental institution in an atmosphere of intellectual exchange. At the age of twenty he found himself living a life in which thinking and its influence had major importance.

153

Three years later he was meeting great men such as Henry Cavendish, Count Rumford, and Sir Joseph Banks, as a lecturer at the famous Royal Institution, where his point of view had some weight.

The accomplishments of others had served to goad Davy's own ambitions. He incessantly hammered his laboratory with questions. His deductions show how quickly he could go from hypothesis to experiment to conclusion. Certainly his lectures had been successful. Nor was Davy unaware that the annual lectures on agriculture, in 1813, were the only systematic investigation in that area. He knew his work on voltaic cells was revolutionary.

Davy also came to shrewd conclusions concerning what he observed. He realized through what he perceived in the action of simple cells that it must be due to substances having opposite charges that electrolysis was possible at all. Davy thought this must mean that all substances could be decomposed by electrolysis into the elements of which they were made. It is this work which led directly to his isolation of sodium and potassium from the alkalies in 1807.

His studies of chlorine show great astuteness. His work demonstrated the correct relation of chlorine to hydrochloric acid and he was able to explain the bleaching action of chlorine. The studies of chlorine resolved great differences of opinion among Swedish, French, and British chemists.

Assessment of Davy's Contributions

There is more than enough for a lasting fame in Davy's work. Yet he would have been troubled to realize how close he came to the mainstream of other great ideas in science. During the discomforts of his illness and in his memories of the suffering patients at the Pneumatic Institution in Bristol, he would have been startled to learn how close he came to the possibility that anesthesia could be used in surgery. Davy was also a small part of the battle against caloric in the development of the modern theory of heat. Count Rumford's great work in 1798 on the generation of heat by friction was to lead to the work of Mayer and Joule in 1840.

John Dalton's work in 1808 on atomic theory, which Davy held in apparent ill regard, was based partly on Humphry Davy's discovery of sodium and potassium that same year.

Davy's is also the massive step between Volta and Faraday in electrochemistry, and it was in extending Davy's methods systematically that Faraday proved that the passage of a current through a liquid would dissociate the liquid at the two electrodes in an accurate, predictable, repeatable manner.

And there is always Michael Faraday.

How can we measure the influence of Davy, through the even greater scientific accomplishments of Michael Faraday? Faraday himself, despite the attacks Davy leveled at him, frequently acknowledged his great debt to his teacher and tutor.

Davy's writings set patterns for experimental investigation that were very necessary to the coming surge of scientific study. If he had been able to succeed in his ambitious plans to write a complete "Elements of Chemical Philosophy," we have the word of the great Swedish scientist Berzelius that it would have advanced the science of chemistry a full century.

The pathways of science are diverse, and those in which Humphry Davy worked were left smoother and clearer because of his accomplishments.

Index

Index

Index

Index

Index